ESSENTIAL LIFE SKILLS FOR TEEN BOYS

A Guide to Managing
Your Home, Health,
Money, and Routine
for an Independent Life

DANI SILAS

**Producer & International Distributor
eBookPro Publishing**
www.ebook-pro.com

ESSENTIAL LIFE SKILLS FOR TEEN BOYS: A Guide to Managing Your Home, Health, Money, and Routine for an Independent Life

DANI SILAS

Copyright © 2023 Made Easy Press

All rights reserved; No parts of this book may be reproduced or transmitted in any form or by any means, electronic or mechanical, including photocopying, recording, taping, or by any information retrieval system, without the permission, in writing, of the author.

Illustrations and Cover: Natalie Lukatsky

Contact: agency@ebook-pro.com
ISBN 9789655753585

CONTENTS

INTRODUCTION 5

PART 1: AROUND THE KITCHEN

    CHAPTER 1: Introduction to Kitchen Appliances....... 8

    CHAPTER 2: The Food Groups...................... 12

    CHAPTER 3: Shopping for Groceries................ 14

    CHAPTER 4: Following a Recipe................... 17

    CHAPTER 5: Basic Recipes 20

    CHAPTER 6: Meal Prepping 24

PART 2: AT HOME

    CHAPTER 7: Cleaning Equipment 30

    CHAPTER 8: Cleaning a Bathroom 34

    CHAPTER 8: Household Maintenance Tools 36

    CHAPTER 10: Household Repairs 39

    CHAPTER 11: Doing Laundry 42

    CHAPTER 12: Ironing 46

PART 3: PERSONAL HEALTH AND CARE

    CHAPTER 13: Healthy Eating 50

    CHAPTER 14: Basic First Aid.................... 53

    CHAPTER 15: Personal Hygiene................... 56

    CHAPTER 16: Sleeping Well 59

    CHAPTER 17: Wardrobe Essentials 62

PART 4: MONEY AND BUDGETING

CHAPTER 18: Planning a Budget 66
CHAPTER 19: Saving Up 70
CHAPTER 20: Taxes 73
CHAPTER 21: Credit Score 76

PART 5: SOCIAL SKILLS

CHAPTER 22: Emergency Contacts 80
CHAPTER 23: Basic Etiquette 82
CHAPTER 24: Navigating Social Media 85
CHAPTER 25: Resolving Conflict 88
CHAPTER 26: Having Difficult Conversations 91

PART 6: PERSONAL DEVELOPMENT

CHAPTER 27: Time Management 96
CHAPTER 28: Setting Personal Goals 99
CHAPTER 29: Car Care and Maintenance 103
CHAPTER 30: Basics of Camping 107
CHAPTER 31: Grilling 110

PART 7: WORKING

CHAPTER 32: Writing a Résumé 116
CHAPTER 33: Finding a Job 120
CHAPTER 34: Acing an Interview 123
CHAPTER 35: Understanding Your Paycheck 127

CONCLUSION 130

INTRODUCTION

Growing up and gaining your independence is one of the most exciting times in your life. You're just starting to figure yourself out, you're developing hopes and dreams for your future and you have so much to enjoy and look forward to.

However, as a teen, it's understandable if you sometimes feel frustrated that you don't yet have all the knowledge or skills you need to truly go out and take the world by storm. Schools do a good job teaching you math, science, and literature, which are all very important things to know. But what about those little things in day-to-day life that no one ever bothered to teach you?

Knowing your way around the kitchen, for instance, and preparing basic meals. Budgeting your money so that you can save up for future expenses. Even learning to take care of a car or how to navigate social media.

This book lets you take your life into your own hands and covers all the big and small things you should know as a young adult.

You can read it from cover to cover, or you can skip between select topics. In a jam and suddenly need to iron a shirt? Jump straight to chapter 12. Having some thoughts about getting a car and looking for help getting started? Open up chapter 29. Ready to go out and get your first job but have no idea how to approach writing your résumé? Chapter 32 has exactly what you need.

That's the beauty of learning life skills – you can learn them any way at any time, and chances are all the skills in this book are ones you will put to good use some day. If not today, maybe in a year or two, or perhaps not even until you're an adult! But each and every one will enrich your knowledge and improve your ability to be a confident, self-sufficient human.

Remember – being a teenager is the perfect time to take risks and try new things. Use this book as a friendly guide to taking your first steps in the big wide world, where endless opportunity and adventure await!

PART 1:

AROUND THE KITCHEN

CHAPTER 1:
INTRODUCTION TO KITCHEN APPLIANCES

The kitchen is an integral part of any home and an important thing to get to know as you become an adult. The kitchen is where you store your food and prepare your meals, so it's crucial to know your way around it.

REFRIGERATOR AND FREEZER

These are essential appliances in every kitchen. Refrigerators have a regulated temperature that is lower than room temperature, usually between 37°-41°F, and it is ideal for storing perishable foods.

This includes fruits and vegetables, dairy products such as milk, cheese, and yogurts, eggs, fresh fish and meat (if intended to be cooked soon), drinks, and condiments.

Freezers are kept at a lower temperature, usually below 0°F. Foods stored in the freezer will freeze within a few hours, so keep this in mind when planning your meals – you might have to defrost something before you can use it!

MICROWAVE

A microwave is an appliance used to defrost or heat food, and sometimes even for cooking meals. Microwaves are quick and easy to use, making them an efficient kitchen appliance. Use the time and power settings on the microwave to best heat your food. Some microwaves also have a "defrost" setting, which is perfect for quick and easy defrosting.

OVEN

Ovens are mainly used for cooking, heating food, and baking. The temperature of the oven can be set to preference and usually ranges between 200°-400°F. Lower temperatures are ideal for defrosting and heating food, medium temperatures are used for cooking and baking and higher temperatures mainly serve for short-term roasting.

Oven-safe cookware includes copper, steel, cast iron, and non-stick. Most pots, pans, and baking trays are okay in the oven. Dishes that are not oven-safe include wood, plastic, and ceramic.

Ovens have different settings, each for different uses. These are the most commonly used oven settings:

- **CONVENTIONAL** – the oven will heat both on the top and the bottom, eliciting a uniform temperature. This setting is used for meats, bread, and some cakes.

- **BOTTOM ELEMENT** – only the bottom element of the oven will heat up. This is good for things that need a crispy base.

- **FAN** – this setting uses a fan to spread hot air throughout the oven. It is suitable for large dishes which need to be soft on the inside but well done on the outside, like cakes and meats that are rare on the inside.

- **GRILL** – wavy lines indicate a grill setting, which is best for crisping and browning food. Use it for toasted sandwiches, cheesy casseroles like lasagna, and roasted vegetables.
- **BOTTOM ELEMENT WITH GRILL** – this is a good function for pies, quiches, and pizzas.
- **FAN GRILL** – the fan distributes heat evenly while the grill roasts from the top. Perfect for cooking meat and poultry.

STOVETOP

A stovetop can be gas, electric, or induction. Stovetops are used for cooking and frying in pots and pans. Gas cooktops use an open flame which can be adjusted instantly. Electric stovetops use heating elements encased in ceramic-glass surfaces, on which dishes can be placed directly. Induction stovetops use electromagnetic energy to generate heat directly within cookware, essentially making the dishes heat themselves. Induction cooktops can only be used with compatible dishes – so always check to make sure your pot or pan is induction-safe.

DISHWASHER

A dishwasher, while not found in every kitchen, is a useful time-saving appliance. It uses a mixture of water and detergent distributed by rotating sprayers, saving you the effort of hand-washing your dishes. It is important to check that your dishes are dishwasher-safe. Cast iron, wood, and non-stick are examples of what you should *not* put in your dishwasher.

When using a dishwasher, make sure to always place hollow dishes (like cups and bowls) upside down. Don't forget to load the dishwasher detergent, which can come in the form of tablets, powder, or gel. Do not use regular dish soap in your dishwasher! Next, choose the wash cycle you want – quick (for fewer dishes that are not too dirty), normal, or heavy-duty (for heavily soiled dishes).

TIPS

- When storing cooked food in the fridge, always make sure to store it in sealed containers. This will keep your fridge from picking up odors which can be hard to eliminate, and will also serve to make sure your food stays fresh for longer.
- You must never put anything with metal in it in a microwave – metal igniting in a microwave is a common cause of kitchen fires. This includes aluminum foil.
- When following a recipe that calls to use an oven, always make sure to set the mode and temperature according to the recipe's requirements.

Now you have a working understanding of the appliances in your kitchen, what each one does, and how to use them.

In the following chapters, we'll get into the next steps – knowing which food to buy and how to maintain a healthy lifestyle.

CHAPTER 2:

THE FOOD GROUPS

All of the food we eat can be categorized into five main food groups. Each food group has its nutritious benefits, and it is important to consume a balanced diet that includes all five food groups.

FRUITS

The fruit group includes all fruits and 100% fruit juice. Fruits have numerous health benefits and provide important nutrients. They can be eaten fresh, pureed, cooked, or in many other forms. You can incorporate fruit into your meals in smoothies, salads, or even fruit juices.

VEGETABLES

Vegetables are nutrient-dense and a good source of vitamins and minerals. This food group includes vegetables, beans, and legumes – like peas, lentils, and chickpeas. Incorporating vegetables into most of your meals is a nutritious, healthy habit.

GRAINS

The grains food group includes foods made from wheat, rice, oats, barley, or any other cereal grain – bread, pasta, rice, oatmeal, popcorn, and breakfast cereals are all considered grains. Grains can be whole or refined – some whole grains are whole wheat, oatmeal, and brown rice. Refined grains include white flour and white rice. Whole grains are considered a healthier choice as they contain more fiber, vitamins, minerals, and antioxidants than refined foods.

PROTEIN

Proteins are important in building muscles, cartilage, skin, and blood cells, thanks to the many nutrients they provide. Proteins fall into six sub-categories:

1. **LEAN MEATS** – like beef, lamb, veal, and pork
2. **POULTRY** – chicken, turkey, duck, etc.
3. **FISH AND SEAFOOD**
4. **EGGS**
5. **NUTS AND SEEDS**
6. **LEGUMES AND BEANS** – which are also considered part of the vegetables food group.

DAIRY

Dairy foods, like milk, yogurt, and cheese, are an important source of calcium, vitamin A, and vitamin D. They are vital for maintaining strong bones and keeping your body healthy. Milk products are popularly used in breakfast foods but can be incorporated into any meal – in salads, casseroles, sandwiches, and even hot or cold drinks.

In chapter 13, *Healthy Eating*, we will review the food groups in greater detail and learn how to put together healthy, nutritious meals that are also delicious.

CHAPTER 3:
SHOPPING FOR GROCERIES

Going grocery shopping can seem like a daunting task, especially when you shop at big supermarkets. But with the right tips and information, navigating the aisles and stocking your fridge and pantry can be a breeze!

First things first – start by making a list. Look through your fridge, freezer, pantry, and any other place you store food, and make a note of whatever you're running low on. A useful way to keep track of things that have run out or are about to run out is to keep a running list up on the fridge and document anything you notice should be restocked throughout the week. That way, you'll be less likely to miss out on important things when you prepare your final shopping list.

Don't forget to also consider any other household items you may need, such as toiletries and cleaning supplies. Dividing your list into sections such as fruits and vegetables, dairy, condiments, baked goods, freezer, and pantry can help you orient yourself when you get to the grocery store and save precious time.

Creating a menu for the coming week can help you construct your shopping list in the most efficient way. We'll talk some more about this in chapter 6, *Meal Prepping*.

Next, plan a budget. Make sure your budget is flexible, as you will have different things to buy each week, but it is useful to have a ballpark figure of what you can afford to spend each week on groceries. This will help you avoid overspending and stick to what you need.

When you get to the grocery store, take a minute to figure out the layout. Ideally, you want to go through the aisles systematically and avoid running back and forth to get things you forgot. If you know in advance where each department is, it will be easier to stay focused.

Try to start with the things that will not be damaged if they are in the bottom of your cart or basket – such as freezer items and dry pantry items. Fruits, vegetables, and dairy products are best left for the end so that they can sit on top of the other groceries and avoid getting crushed.

If you're using a shopping cart, you can place eggs and other breakable things in the upper section where kids sit.

As you go through the aisles, look out for special offers or sales. Different brands can offer different prices for the same product – just always make sure to compare by price per quantity, not by overall price. You might see a jar of pasta sauce that is cheaper than another, but if the quantities are not the same it may not be a bargain after all!

Make sure to prepare your payment method in advance. Grocery shopping can be expensive, especially if you're maintaining your own home, so if you plan on paying with cash – make sure you have enough.

When checking out, try to bag your groceries in a way that will make it easier to unpack them at home. Divide your groceries according to where they will go when you get home – freezer items together, fridge items in another bag, fruit and vegetables separate, etc.

TIPS

- Don't go shopping on an empty stomach – this can lead to impulse buying which is never good for your budget.

- Make note of expiration dates when you buy dairy and meat products. You don't want to return home only to discover your milk expires tomorrow!

- Buying in bulk can save money, but make sure only to do this with non-perishable groceries.

CHAPTER 4:

FOLLOWING A RECIPE

Now that you have a working understanding of the different food groups and an idea of how to approach grocery shopping, it's time to learn some essential culinary basics for surviving life as an adult.

Once you've understood how to follow a recipe and mastered the basics, which you'll learn in the next chapter, *Basic Recipes*, you should be able to cook almost anything in the kitchen!

FOLLOWING A RECIPE

Recipes can be found online, in a recipe book, or even scribbled on a piece of paper that's been handed down for generations. At first glance, a recipe can seem quite intimidating – but once you understand its different parts and how to approach them it's super simple.

RECIPES USUALLY HAVE THREE PARTS:

1. *General information* – the name of the dish, the type of cuisine (Italian, Mexican, Chinese, etc.), how many people it serves, and how long it takes to prepare.

   It's easy to pick up a recipe and jump right into making it, but taking a moment to look closely at the details can help you be more prepared. If the dish makes four portions but you need to feed eight people, you'll want to double the amount of each ingredient. You might choose a recipe and then discover that it needs to rest in the fridge for two hours before it is ready, or freeze overnight – which is not ideal if you're looking for a quick dinner fix.

2. *Ingredients* – this is a complete list of all the ingredients you will need to make the dish. It should include everything from protein and grains to herbs, spices, and water.

Before you start, check that you have all the ingredients you need. That way you can avoid getting stuck in the middle of a recipe when you discover you do not have a critical component. Some recipes will suggest possible substitutions – for example, a recipe that calls for milk may note that you can use plant-based milk instead, or another recipe might suggest lower-fat substitutions to make the dish healthier.

Put out all of the ingredients in front of you before you begin. This will help you make sure that you do indeed have everything you need before starting, and will also help you track what you've used to double-check that you haven't missed any step of the instructions.

3. *Directions* – this is a step-by-step list of actions and commands for putting the meal together. This list will always be chronological, so follow it carefully one by one, without skipping between steps.

Just like with the ingredients, read through all of the directions before you start to cook! A recipe that needs baking or cooking time in the oven will let you know what temperature you need to heat the oven to right at the beginning so that you can preheat it in advance. You may look at the directions for another recipe and discover that you need a whisk or a spatula, or another form of kitchenware that isn't immediately available to you.

Once you've mastered the skill of following a recipe, there is literally nothing you can't try. There are endless options for breakfast, lunch, dinner, snacks, and desserts – just waiting for you to tackle.

CHAPTER 5:
BASIC RECIPES

Now, let's go over some basic recipes for dishes you should definitely master in your teens. Remember the guidelines from the last chapter about how to correctly follow a recipe!

MAKING PASTA . . . .

Pasta

Cuisine: Italian | Serves: 6 | Total time: 25 minutes

Ingredients:

1 pound (500g) dry pasta

Cold water

1 tbsp. (tablespoon) kosher salt

Directions:

1. Fill a big pot with water.
2. Place the pot on the stovetop on the highest heat.
3. While the water is heating, stir in the salt until it has completely dissolved.
4. Once the water is boiling (remember, this is when bubbles begin to form on the surface), pour in the pasta.
5. Lower the heat to medium and stir the pasta from time to time, cooking according to the directions on the package – usually between 8 and 12 minutes.
6. Once the pasta has cooked, remove the pot from the heat and carefully drain the pasta.
7. You can add any sauce you like or rinse it to cool and then use it in a salad or casserole

BOILING AN EGG

Eggs are a very versatile ingredient and a good source of protein for any meal. They can be fried or made into omelets, baked into pies or quiches, or incorporated into a salad. A boiled egg can be eaten as a side dish, in a salad, or in a sandwich, the possibilities are endless.

BOILED EGGS

Serves: 1
Total time: 30 minutes

INGREDIENTS:

- 2 eggs
- Cold water
- Ice (optional)

DIRECTIONS:

1. Fill a small pot with cold water and place your eggs in the pot. Make sure that the eggs are completely submerged in the water.

2. Put the pot on the stovetop on high heat. Watch over the pot until you see bubbles forming on the surface of the water – this is your sign that the water has boiled.

3. Once the water has boiled, cover the pot with a lid and remove it from the stovetop, setting it aside.

4. Set a timer for 10 minutes – this is the recommended cooking time for a hard-boiled egg. For a soft-boiled egg that is still runny inside, set the timer for 4-6 minutes.

5   While you wait, fill a bowl with cold water and ice. If you don't have ice, you can just use cold water.

6   Once the time is up, remove the lid from the pot and carefully take out the eggs using a large spoon or tongs. Place them in the bowl of cold water and allow them to cool for 10 minutes.

7   Tap the eggs gently on a hard surface to crack the shell and then peel. Your eggs are ready!

MAKING A SALAD

Ok, so a salad isn't really technically cooking. Still, salad is a healthy, nutritious, versatile, and quick meal option, which is why it is one of the most important basic recipes to learn how to make. There are so many different types of salads you can put together once you are familiar with the basic guidelines to make sure you have a salad that is delicious and filling.

Salads are (usually) cold dishes made from chopped ingredients, most of which are vegetables, and tossed with dressing.

HERE ARE INSTRUCTIONS FOR MAKING A SALAD THAT DOESN'T SUCK:

1   Start with leafy greens. Lettuce, kale, fresh spinach leaves, arugula, or cabbage make a great, crispy salad base. Choose one or combine two or more!

2   Add your favorite vegetables. You can use cucumbers, tomatoes, peppers, carrots, onions, beets, mushrooms, celery, or anything else you like. You can add the vegetables

fresh or you can boil or grill them. Examples of vegetables that grill well are carrots, peppers, zucchini, beets, and mushrooms.

3. Add a protein. Choose a cold protein such as salty cheese, canned or fresh tuna, beans, lentils, tofu, a boiled egg, chicken, cooked or smoked salmon, etc. Protein makes your salad more filling and nutritious, and of course – more delicious.

4. Next, add grains. Incorporating grains into your salad helps to round it out nutritiously and will keep you full for longer. Popular salad grains are quinoa, bulgur, couscous, pasta, croutons, or seeds. Opt for whole grains if you're looking for a healthier option.

5. Finally, finish with a salad dressing. You can go for a simple olive oil and lemon juice dressing, use a ready-made Italian vinaigrette, or get creative and make your own dressing. There are plenty of healthy, delicious recipes you can find online!

You can experiment with your salads, devising your favorite recipes and eating them for lunch or dinner, or even breakfast! You can even prep salads in advance for busy days, which you'll learn about in the next chapter, Meal Prepping.

CHAPTER 6:

MEAL PREPPING

The last chapters have taught you some basic skills in the kitchen – how to use various appliances, how to incorporate the different food groups into your diet, how to follow a recipe, and some basic recipes to get you started.

If you're interested in taking your cooking and kitchen skills up a notch, the next thing you can try is food prepping! Food prepping is the practice of preparing whole meals in advance and in bulk, to save precious time during the week.

Imagine that you have a busy day at school or work and won't have time to cook lunch or dinner. You don't want to eat out again because that's expensive and you're doing your best to save. Then, you open your fridge to see neatly stacked, healthy, nutritious meals ready to take with you or eat on the go!

Meal prepping saves time, it saves money, and it is an efficient way to eat healthy without making too much of an effort and to reduce the stress of cooking on busy days.

So, how to meal prep?

The basic idea is that instead of cooking one meal at a time, you utilize one cooking session to prepare multiple meals which you can eat for the next few days.

First, decide which meals you'd like to prepare in advance. Perhaps you leave home early in the morning and don't have time to make a healthy breakfast. Maybe you don't eat at the school cafeteria and want to prepare lunches for school days. Or maybe you simply need some nutritious snacks to take with you for long days out of the house.

Then, find some time to make the meals. The best time for this is on the weekend when you can dedicate a concentrated hour or two to save you time later.

Before you begin, make sure you have all the ingredients you need. You can jump back to chapter 3 for a reminder on how to approach grocery shopping.

Invest in some good food containers that are sealed and durable so that you can dish out the meals you've prepared and keep them neatly in the fridge or freezer.

Here are some ideas for meals you can prep in advance:

BREAKFAST

- **OVERNIGHT OATS** – fill a bowl or jar with raw oats, milk of your choice, and fruit, and keep sealed in the fridge for an easy breakfast. You can add things like yogurt, chia seeds, honey, cocoa, or anything that comes to mind.
- **BREAKFAST MUFFINS** – egg or cheese-based, these are great for grabbing on the way out the door.
- **SMOOTHIE** – if you cut and prep all the vegetables and fruit and then keep them in the freezer in labeled bags, all you have to do on a busy morning is throw the ingredients into the blender, add liquid, and voila – breakfast is ready.

- **HOMEMADE GRANOLA BARS** – healthy and delicious, these are a great choice if you're looking for a more ambitious way to prep your breakfasts for the week.

LUNCH / DINNER

- Chicken breast with rice or mashed potatoes and grilled vegetables.
- Spaghetti with bolognese or meatballs.
- Taco bowl – ground beef, rice, tomatoes, corn, beans, and avocado with tortilla chips on the side.
- Deconstructed burrito – pack all the fillings and the burrito separately and then wrap the burrito when you're ready to eat.
- Buddha bowl – a usually vegetarian one-bowl meal with a grain (rice, quinoa), protein (tofu, chickpeas, beans), and vegetables (fresh or roasted).
- Stir fry packed with vegetables and the protein of your choice and served on whole grain (rice or noodles work great!).

SNACKS

- Homemade trail mix – use a mixture of nuts, seeds, and fruit as your base, and then add ingredients to your heart's content – chocolate, coconut, pretzels, peanut butter chips, etc.
- Dates filled with walnuts or pecans and coated in dark chocolate.

- Edamame.
- Smoothies (great for a snack as well as breakfast!)
- Crackers with cheese and vegetable strips.
- Granola bars – you can make these at home or buy your favorites in the supermarket.

PART 2:

AT HOME

CHAPTER 7:

CLEANING EQUIPMENT

A big part of being an adult is learning how to look after your own space and clean up after yourself. This handy introduction to the most basic and commonly used cleaning equipment and tools that can be found in almost any home is a great start.

First – tools. Here is a rundown of all the standard tools you need to keep a house clean.

BROOM AND DUSTPAN

These are essential for quick clean-ups of dry spills, or for preparing your space before vacuuming and cleaning the floor. Don't use a broom on wet spills, like water or mud, but for cleaning up spilled cereal, broken glass, or debris these are your go-to tools.

VACUUM

A vacuum is an incredibly effective tool for keeping dust at bay and eliminating dirt from the floor and other surfaces. Some vacuum cleaners are wireless while others must be connected to electricity to use. There are also automatic vacuum cleaners that work on a schedule, completely autonomously. Make sure not to vacuum up anything that can damage the machine, like shards of glass – it's better to deal with those using a broom and dustpan.

BUCKET AND MOP

Once your floors are swept or vacuumed, they need to be washed. Grab a bucket, fill it with warm water and cleaning fluid, and use your mop to distribute the cleaning solution evenly over the floor. Once the floor has been washed, it will take some time to dry. Try not to walk around on the floor when it's wet, as you can end up leaving stains that will tarnish your beautiful, clean home.

A bucket is also useful for rinsing out sponges or rags and for storing your cleaning equipment between uses.

Make sure never to use regular cleaning fluid and water on wooden parquet floors – these floors need special treatment and materials specifically designed for parquet so as not to damage the wood.

TOILET BRUSH

Toilets need to be cleaned regularly, so a designated toilet brush is an important investment. These usually come on a long handle, with a small stand where you can put your cleaning solution while using it.

GOOD SPONGES

Sponges are a versatile and incredibly useful cleaning tool. They can be used to scrub surfaces, walls, and even stubborn dirt on floors. Opt for sponges that have one rough side and one soft side, for an even more adaptable cleaning tool.

MICROFIBER CLEANING CLOTHS

These are great for picking up dust and wiping down delicate surfaces, like wood. They can also be used to clean windows, mirrors, or screens with the right cleaning solutions.

Next – cleaning solutions! There are many different types and brands, but here are some guidelines of what to use and when.

There are four different types of cleaning agents: detergents, degreasers, abrasives, and acids.

DETERGENTS

These are the most gentle solutions, and the most commonly used in homes. Detergents come in various forms – sprays, gels, powders, and more, and usually need to be added to water in order to work. These are best used for cleaning everyday spills and dirt.

DEGREASERS

These are, as their name indicates, solutions that battle grease, oils, and stubborn organic messes. You use them to clean ovens, stovetops, and even greasy cookware – although make sure your degreaser is food-safe before you use it on dishes.

ABRASIVES

These cleaning agents are more powerful than detergents and are used to clean dirt from hard surfaces. These are less common in households and are used more in commercial settings.

ACIDS

Acids can be mild or strong, but it is always best to wear gloves when using them. These are found most commonly in products used for cleaning toilets and showers, as they are very strong and can easily break down difficult stains.

TIPS

- Use gloves whenever you work with bleach or more powerful cleaning agents, to keep your hands safe and to prevent damaging your skin.

In chapter 8, we'll get right into the nitty-gritty of the proper way to clean a bathroom.

CHAPTER 8:

CLEANING A BATHROOM

The bathroom is one of the most important rooms in the house to keep clean and sanitary. It is where you shower, relieve yourself, brush your teeth, and get ready in the morning, and we rely on it to keep us clean – so it goes without saying that it should be impeccably clean.

Keeping a bathroom clean, besides being important, is also somewhat more complicated than keeping other rooms clean. The water, steam, and general dampness of a bathroom can easily make it a breeding ground for fungus, bacteria, mildew, and even mold, which is why it is crucial to practice good hygiene habits and clean the bathroom at least once a week.

Follow these steps on cleaning day to ensure that your bathroom and everything in it stays fresh and sanitary:

1. Clear the surfaces. Remove anything you might have on the sink – toothbrush and toothpaste, soap, creams, deodorant, etc. – and anything sitting on the bathtub or in the shower – body soap, shampoo, conditioner – as well as anything that may be on the floor, like a trash can or bathmat. Toss your towels in the laundry.

2. Remove dust from shelves, towel racks or hooks, windowsills, electric outlets (carefully), light switches, walls, and any other dusty surfaces.

3. Start with the sink and vanity. Spray the surfaces with a cleaning solution and then scrub with a sponge and wipe

them down with paper or cloth. Spray the mirror with window spray and wipe it with a microfiber towel until it shines.

4. Use an all-purpose cleaner to scrub the toilet with a toilet brush. For more stubborn stains, you can use bleach – but don't forget to put on gloves beforehand. Scrub the inside of the toilet as well as the rim and seat. Flush the toilet and wipe down the seat to finish.

5. Next, move on to the bath or shower. Spray a cleaning solution over the entire surface of the bath, shower floor, doors, and tiles. Let it rest for a few minutes and then rinse off with the shower head, taking care not to soak the bathroom floor. Mold or mildew can be tackled with a heavier cleaning solution, such as bleach or another acid-based solution, and a sponge (remember gloves!).

6. Finally, get to work on the floor. You may need to sweep or vacuum first, but once the floor is clear fill a bucket with warm water and floor cleaning solution. Use a mop or cloth to distribute the water all over the floor, getting into tight spaces like under the sink or behind the toilet.

7. Finally, replace the towels and/or bathmat with new, fresh ones and put everything back tidily on the vanity. For a finishing touch, you can spray the bathroom with an air freshener, add a toilet bowl freshener that clips onto the seat, and put a new bag in the trash can. Refill any soap dispensers that need refilling and replenish your toilet paper and other necessities.

After following these steps, your bathroom should be perfectly spotless and ready to be used!

CHAPTER 8:

HOUSEHOLD MAINTENANCE TOOLS

Homes require constant love and care, and periodical maintenance work.

Some maintenance is best left to professionals who know what they are doing and are skilled at their craft, but there are certainly little maintenance jobs you can take care of around the house – things like changing light bulbs, hanging pictures and shelves, patching holes in the walls, and more.

To tackle these tasks, you need to have the proper equipment handy. Here is a list of some household tools you should have on hand in case of an emergency, and what each one can be used for.

HAMMER AND NAILS

Whether you need to hang something up on a wall or put together a piece of furniture, a hammer and nails are your number one household tool. Hammers can range in size and shape, but for simple tasks, a relatively light hammer with a regular head is perfectly sufficient. Nails are a hammer's best friend – they are long with flat heads and are meant to be hammered directly into drywall, wood, or other softer surfaces.

SCREWDRIVER AND SCREWS

You should have a screwdriver available in your toolbox at all times. The most use you will find for it is probably tightening loose screws in anything from cabinets and door hinges to furniture and kitchen appliances. Use a Phillips screwdriver when your screw has an X-shape on the top, and a flat screwdriver when you're working with a screw that has a straight line across the top.

It's best to also keep a collection of screws of different sizes, lengths, and shapes, in case you need to replace a screw that has broken or rusted, or for simple construction projects.

WD-40

WD-40 is a multi-functional oil-based formula that can be used for many things around the home. It comes in a spray can and can be used to protect tools from corrosion, lubricate squeaky hinges and wheels, loosen screws, remove rust, and more.

SPIRIT LEVEL

When hanging pictures, shelves, cabinets, or other decorative elements, it is important to make sure they are straight and parallel to the floor. A spirit level is a recommended tool for your toolbox, as it is easily utilized and very accurate. Once you've positioned what you wish to hang, simply place the spirit level on top of it and watch for the bubble. When the bubble is perfectly centered, your item is level.

TAPE MEASURE

A tape measure is a long, flexible ruler used for measuring lengths and distances. They are compact and easy to store but stretch out to anything from one to three meters for accurate and easy measuring. Its flexibility allows you to measure awkward shapes and spaces, and even around corners, making it an essential addition to your collection of household tools. Tape measures often have a metal clip attached to the end so that you can fasten them wherever you want – helpful when you're working alone!

STEP LADDER

A step ladder doesn't need much explanation – it's useful for reaching places you wouldn't be able to reach on your own. When hanging things high up on a wall or changing a light bulb on the ceiling, it's best to have a stable step ladder or stool to stand on, rather than relying on other less stable, and more dangerous, pieces of furniture.

TIPS

- Keep all of your tools tidy in a toolbox, bag, or designated drawer – this will make them easier to locate in times of need.

CHAPTER 10:
HOUSEHOLD REPAIRS

There are all sorts of odd household jobs and repairs that self-sufficient teens and adults should know how to take care of on their own so that they can avoid wasting time and money on hiring a professional. Of course, there are things you should never attempt to do yourself – like plumbing, anything to do with electricity or gas, or more complicated renovations. You should definitely seek a professional's help for any of these, but things like patching a hole in the wall, changing a light bulb, or unclogging a drain are certainly within your abilities!

REPLACING A LIGHT BULB.....................

Changing a light bulb is one of the easiest repairs you can do around the house. Bulbs lose power now and then and usually need to be replaced quite quickly, as it is difficult to maintain your routine in a dark house or room.

1. Find out which bulb you need. Light bulbs come in different sizes, colors, and shapes, so you need to be aware of your options. Make sure the bulb you buy is the same size and wattage as the one you're removing (the details should be written on the bulb itself and the packaging) and choose whether you prefer a yellow or white light.

2. Before you do anything, turn off the power. Trying to change a light that is connected to electricity can be very dangerous!

3. Make sure the bulb is cool before you remove it. Twist it out of its fixture carefully, holding onto it from its base, not from the glass.

4. Fit in the new bulb. Again, twist it carefully until you feel resistance.

5. Step away from the fixture and turn the power back on. It is best to keep a safe distance just in case there is a short circuit or the bulb falls out of its place.

PATCHING A HOLE IN THE WALL

When we hang things on walls, like pictures, hooks, shelves, or mirrors, the hanging process usually causes some damage to the wall. This damage isn't visible as long as the item is still hanging, but when we remove it for any reason – moving house, renovations, redecorating – that damage can suddenly become an eyesore that no one wants to see.

So how do we patch a hole in the wall left behind by a nail or screw?

1. First, use sandpaper or another rough surface to smooth over the surface around the hole. You don't want to have any sharp or rugged edges that will be difficult to patch over.

2. Next, get your spackling or drywall compound ready. These come in small or large buckets and can be found in most building supply stores and some department stores. Use a small knife or scraper to gently fill the hole with the compound. Smooth the edges flat so they are level with the wall.

3. Leave the wall to dry for a few hours.

4. Finally, once it's dry, sand it down again. If the wall is painted you will have to paint over the space you're filled in so it matches the rest of the wall.

UNCLOGGING A DRAIN

Sink, bathtub, and shower drains sometimes get clogged up due to residue, hairs, or food substances that get stuck inside. You will know you have a clogged drain when you notice that the water is draining more slowly than usual, or not at all. Unclogging a drain is an easy fix!

1. First, try a simple white vinegar and baking soda solution. Mix one part vinegar and one part baking soda (about ¼ of a cup each) in a bowl until they fizz. Pour the solution down the drain immediately and let it sit for an hour at least. The chemical reaction between the substances should break down most of the gunk clogged in the drain. Then, pour boiling water down the drain to finish off the job.

2. If that doesn't work, you may have to manually remove whatever is stuck. You can use a wire hanger or plunger to carefully extract whatever is blocking the water.

3. With baths or showers, you might have to use a stronger commercial unclogging solution to clear out the drain.

If none of these solutions work – it's time to call a plumber who has more tools and the know-how to deal with stubborn drains.

CHAPTER 11:

DOING LAUNDRY

Laundry is one of those household chores that if you're not taught how to do correctly, you may well end up doing wrong. And doing laundry wrong often means saying a sad goodbye to treasured garments or comfy favorites. With this laundry guide for beginners and the helpful tips laid out at the end, you'll be sure to get your laundry right every single time!

SORTING YOUR LAUNDRY

Not all clothes and garments should be washed together. This is why we separate our laundry into separate loads. You can do this in advance, separating loads in different baskets throughout the week, or simply throw everything together and sort the clothes out once you're ready to put them in the washing machine.

Separating whites from colors is the first important step. White or other light-colored garments, when washed with darker clothes, can come out looking grimy, or a different color altogether. Make sure to separate white and light items from the rest.

Some garments are more delicate than others and they should be washed separately as well. These include mainly undergarments, which require a gentler wash cycle.

Other items, like delicate silks, evening gowns, wool, etc., shouldn't be washed in a machine at all – wash these by hand, per the instructions that will follow.

READING A LAUNDRY LABEL

Many pieces of clothing have labels, usually sewn into an inner seam or waistband, with specific instructions on laundering. Check these labels on new clothes to see whether they require special attention.

Here are some commonly-used laundry-related symbols, and what they mean:

  Machine wash – normal setting

  Machine wash – delicate setting

  Machine wash – below 80°F

  Machine wash – below 105°F

  Machine wash – below 120°F

  Machine wash – below 140°F

  Hand wash only

  Do not launder – dry clean only

WASHING AND DRYING

Once your laundry is sorted, you can begin. Before you load your clothes or linens into the washing machine, check them one by one to see if any have stubborn stains. Treat stains before washing by applying stain remover or simply rubbing some laundry detergent into the stain. You might want to consider washing clothes that are more seriously stained by hand. Make sure to unfold any sleeves or cuffs and separate balled-up socks before loading them.

After loading the machine, add detergent and fabric softener according to the machine's instructions. Most washing machines have dispensers in a little drawer that can be pulled out. The detergent will go in the section marked with two lines in a circle. The fabric softener compartment will be marked with a flower.

Detergent can come in the form of powder, liquid gel, or gel capsules. Capsules go directly into the drum together with the clothes.

Next, use the dial or buttons on the machine to choose the appropriate water temperature. The "normal" cycle should be fine for most clothes, but select a colder setting for delicates. Bed sheets and towels should be washed at a higher temperature as they need more of a sanitization treatment.

Take care not to overfill the machine – if the clothes don't have enough place to spin around, they won't come out clean. Leave about a quarter to a third of the space empty.

Once the wash cycle has finished, it's time to dry the clothes. You can either use a dryer or hang the garments out to dry – if the weather is warm enough to allow it.

Never put garments made of silk, leather, suede, wool, or spandex in the dryer, as these can be easily damaged or shrink!

When the dry cycle is complete, remove the clothes and fold them as soon as you can. This will reduce wrinkling and save you precious ironing time later.

HAND WASHING

Delicate or very dirty garments do better hand washed than in the laundry – and as previously mentioned, some clothes have clear instructions on them to hand-wash only.

First, find a clean sink, basin, or large bucket. Fill with lukewarm water – not too cold and not too hot, then add detergent to the mix. Place your clothes in the sink or bucket, preferably one at a time. Scrub them gently by hand, focusing on visibly stained parts. Then, rinse in cold water and observe the garment. It will usually take at least two or three times to make sure your clothes are thoroughly cleaned. Dry as normal.

TIPS

- If you're using a dryer, make sure to empty the lint trap before every use. There should be instructions on the machine explaining where the lint trap is and how to extract it.

- Use a mesh laundry bag to keep your socks together – that way, you'll never end up with single socks!

- Dryer sheets can be placed in the dryer with the clothes and give them a nice, fresh smell when they come out. You can even put used dryer sheets in your closet or sock drawer to keep them fragrant.

CHAPTER 12:

IRONING

Ironing is perhaps one of the more important but lesser-known life skills. Plenty of clothes you wear are perfectly fine without being ironed, but some items of clothing are blatantly obvious when they're not ironed.

Walking around with creased clothes is fine for going out with friends or running errands, but in more formal settings like at work, school, or events where you want to look your best, your outfit should look neat and tidy.

There are some items you should *always* iron, others that need to be ironed depending on the fabric, and others yet that must never be ironed.

THINGS YOU SHOULD ALWAYS IRON

- Button-down shirts
- Chinos
- Fitted garments

In general, fabrics that can be ironed are linen, cotton, denim, polyester, silk, and satin.

THINGS YOU SHOULD NOT IRON

- Wet, dirty, or stained clothes
- Wool or knit sweaters
- Beaded or sequined fabrics
- Velvet

HOW TO IRON

Set up your ironing space. It's best to use an ironing board if you have one, but if not you can use another hard surface. *Never* iron directly on wood, stone, or textiles (like your bedsheet or carpet). You can place a white or other light-colored towel on a surface to protect it from the heat of the iron.

Open up the little flap in the top of the iron and check if there is water inside. If not, fill it with tap or distilled water.

Irons have different heat settings, so start by turning your iron on and setting the temperature according to the item you want to iron. Most clothes have ironing instructions on the label to let you know which setting to use. For most regular clothes that are not delicate, you can use the standard setting. Leave the iron upright (not down on your clothes!) until it reaches the correct temperature.

Spread your clean, laundered garment out on the surface, making sure that it lies flat. Remember, an iron can smooth out creases but it can also create them in the wrong places if your fabric isn't flat.

If you're ironing a shirt, unfold the sleeves and collar and undo the buttons before you start.

Iron your garment carefully, focusing on one part at a time. Press the iron firmly against the fabric, but never leave it in the same place for more than a second, as you can scorch the material. Keep your hand moving over the surface of the garment until it is smooth.

Look for the intentional creases and folds in your garment and hold them in place while you iron. Iron between buttons and around zippers but not directly on them, as they can melt.

Once you've finished, hang or fold the item immediately to avoid creasing.

TIPS

- Clothes that have prints on them or delicate details, like buckles or beads, can be turned inside out to protect them better.

- You can spray a little water on items before ironing them, this will help get the creases out more easily.

- Remove your clothes from the laundry or dryer and iron or fold them as soon as possible. Leaving them crumpled in a heap will only encourage more stubborn creases that will be more difficult to get out later!

PART 3:

PERSONAL HEALTH AND CARE

CHAPTER 13:

HEALTHY EATING

Another important way to take care of yourself as a beginning adult is to take charge of your eating habits and physical health. As you become more independent, the responsibility for planning your meals and snacks and staying healthy becomes yours alone. In this chapter, you will learn the fundamentals of a balanced diet, how to plan a meal, and what different kinds of food and drink can benefit your body's physical wellness.

PUTTING TOGETHER A MEAL . . . .

A healthy, balanced plate has some of everything in it. Vegetables – whether fresh, steamed, canned, or cooked, should comprise about half of your meal. The other half of your plate should include healthy protein, preferably not processed, and grains – preferably whole. You can go back to chapter 2, *The Food Groups*, to refresh your memory about the different food groups and what is included in each.

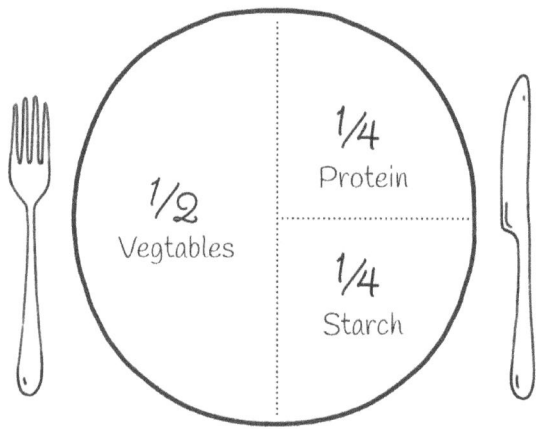

IMPORTANT NUTRIENTS

There are some key nutrients that are incredibly important to integrate into your diet during your teenage years. These nutrients help you keep strong and healthy, and are essential to your bone and muscle development.

IRON helps our cells create hemoglobin, which allows red blood cells to carry oxygen through our bodies. It can be found in proteins like meat and fish, as well as in some plant sources. If you are an active vegetarian or vegan, you'll need to get your iron from other sources so be mindful about consuming iron-rich plant-based foods, like spinach, sweet potatoes, peas, and broccoli.

CALCIUM plays an important role in strengthening bones and teeth and regulating heart rhythms. It is mostly found in dairy products like milk, yogurt, and cheese, but can also be gained through soy, tofu, and even plant-based milk.

VITAMIN D, while not sourced through food, is another crucial nutrient for young bodies. The best way to source vitamin D is through sunlight – which is why finding time to be outside is not only good for your mental health, but for your physical health as well.

HYDRATING

Hydrating regularly, or drinking water, is vital for the health of your internal organs, skin, and hair, and gives you the energy you need to function. Dehydration can lead to fatigue, weakness, muscle cramps, and more.

Remember, you might need to drink even if you don't feel thirsty – so set yourself a daily goal and try to stick to it. A recommended daily amount of water for adults is around eight cups, or more when the weather's hot.

Try to avoid soft drinks with sugar in them, which don't give you the same benefits as drinking water.

TIPS

- Eat a variety of foods – include choices from all the food groups in your meals every day.

- Be active – in addition to eating healthy, getting some activity into your daily routine is extremely important for your physical and mental health. Opt to walk shorter distances instead of driving or taking the bus, play sports as often as you can, and find ways to be active every day.

- Keep a bottle of water on or near you throughout the day to remind you to hydrate regularly.

CHAPTER 14:

BASIC FIRST AID

Knowing how to treat day-to-day injuries with basic first aid is a useful life skill. It allows us to be self-sufficient and independent, instead of relying on others for help with things that are certainly within our capabilities.

In chapter 22, *Emergency Contacts*, we'll go into greater detail about what to do and whom to call when faced with a situation you can't handle on your own, but in this chapter, we'll cover the basics of treating cuts, scrapes, burns, and fever.

ASSEMBLING A FIRST AID KIT

Every young adult should have a well-stocked first aid kit on hand in their home, for emergencies – small and big.

EQUIP YOURSELF with the following things, preferably kept together in an easily accessible location in your home:

- *Band-aids* in a variety of shapes and sizes – for shallow cuts and scrapes

- *Bandages* – for deeper cuts or open wounds that require dressing

- *Sterile gauze dressings*, in a roll or individually packaged

- *Alcohol-free cleansing wipes* – for cleaning and sterilizing injuries before dressing them

- *Antiseptic cream* – for treating mild burns

- *Antibiotic cream*
- *Painkillers*
- *A digital thermometer*
- *Small scissors*
- *Tweezers* – for extracting splinters, glass shards, etc.
- *Safety pins and sticky tape* – for fastening dressings

TREATING CUTS AND SCRAPES

If the injury is bleeding, first clean the blood and press a clean, dry cloth to the wound until the bleeding stops. Then, clean the wound with water or a cleansing wipe and apply antibiotic cream for deeper cuts. When the wound is clean and has stopped bleeding, place a band-aid or bandage over it and secure it tightly in place. Don't forget to change the dressing once or twice a day and whenever it gets wet or dirty.

TREATING A FEVER

The average body temperature in humans is 98.6°F (37°C), and anywhere between 97° and 99°F is considered to be normal. Our body temperature can rise above regular temperature for various causes, most commonly when we are suffering from an infection.

A thermometer is the most effective tool for determining fever. If you notice that your temperature is 101.5°F or higher, or that it hasn't broken for three days, contact your healthcare provider for medical assistance.

Any fever that is lower can be managed at home – make sure to drink lots of fluids to avoid dehydration and keep warm. Painkillers with acetaminophen, ibuprofen, and aspirin can help to lower a fever if you're experiencing discomfort. Always refer to the label for dosage instructions!

TREATING MINOR BURNS

Burns can be painful, but treating them properly and soon after an injury can reduce discomfort immensely. Rinse the burn immediately under cool water for a few minutes, then put on antiseptic cream. Either leave it open to heal, or cover it with gauze if the burn is inconveniently located.

If you have lavender essential oil on hand, you can apply it to a burn and it will reduce the inflammation and relieve your pain.

CHAPTER 15:

PERSONAL HYGIENE

Almost nothing is more important in your day-to-day life than keeping up good hygiene habits. Looking good, smelling nice, and keeping clean is essential to your physical and mental health and, just as importantly, make you pleasant to be around. Some of these habits may seem obvious while others might be new to you, just make sure to incorporate them all into your routine.

SKIN CARE

Our skin is quite sensitive, particularly on our face, neck, and hands, which are the parts of us that are exposed most often. As a teenager, your body goes through changes and your hormones can be unbalanced, causing your skin to be even more sensitive to dryness, oiliness, or acne.

These changes are completely natural and normal and happen to everyone. And while it is almost impossible to avoid them entirely, practicing good skin care habits can reduce to a minimum the short and long-term effects of puberty on your skin.

THESE ARE THINGS YOU SHOULD BE DOING EVERY DAY:

- Wash your face daily with water and a gentle soap. Thoroughly cleanse the skin all over your face and neck, but don't scrub too hard, particularly over areas with acne, as this could cause scarring.

- Apply sunblock to your face and neck (don't forget the back of your neck!) every morning, whether you plan to be out in the sun or not. This will protect your skin and keep it healthy, as well as reduce long-term risks of skin cancer.

DENTAL CARE

As a child, your teeth fall out and change. Once you're a teenager, the teeth in your mouth are there to stay, or in other words – irreplaceable. Practicing good dental hygiene from a young age is necessary to keep your teeth and gums in good condition for years to come.

- Brush your teeth twice a day, every day. Brushing helps to clean your teeth and prevents the buildup of plaque and tartar. Besides staining your teeth, these can also cause gum disease and discomfort if not dealt with. When you brush your teeth every morning and every evening, you rid your mouth of any food particles and stop the plaque from accumulating.

- Floss! Flossing every day in addition to brushing is crucial for your gum health.

- Visit a dentist and dental hygienist at least twice a year for regular checkups and cleaning, and to identify any issues that need to be treated.

- Sugary foods and drinks are detrimental to your dental health, so try to minimize your intake so that you are not eating them every day.

BODY ODOR

It's no secret that teen boys often suffer from bad body odor, which in turn makes it less fun to be around them. This is due again to changing hormones and the process your body is going through in puberty. Also, teen boys tend to be relatively physically active, which doesn't help with cleanliness.

- Make it a habit to shower at least once a day and after any physical exertion. Staying in sweaty clothes is not only unhygienic, but it can also cause irritation to your skin and even infections.

- Wash your hands with soap before and after every meal, after using the bathroom, and whenever else you feel the need.

- Use an antiperspirant regularly – apply it to your armpits after showers and with each change of clothes. This will minimize how much you sweat and also neutralize body odor.

- Bedrooms, especially when they are untidy, can also become stuffy and smell bad. Your privacy is important, but it might mean that your bedroom door is closed most of the time, which doesn't give fresh air a chance to come in and circulate. That is why it is important to keep your room clean and tidy and to air it out by opening a window every so often.

Maintaining good hygiene habits is perhaps one of the more important life skills you will learn, as it is beneficial to your health, both mental and physical, your relationships, and your future.

CHAPTER 16:

SLEEPING WELL

Sleep may seem like a trivial thing, and definitely not something you need to learn how to do – after all, you've been sleeping every night since you were a baby!

While that is true, between the ages of 13 and 18 the *amount* you sleep and the *way* you sleep, or in short, your sleeping habits, can have a huge impact on the quality of your life. Learning healthy and effective sleep habits can be a life-changing skill that can accompany you into adulthood.

There are all sorts of elements in your life, besides tiredness and concentration, that you might not realize are directly related to how much you sleep – such as long and short-term memory, physical and emotional development, brain function, academic achievement, anxiety, and creativity.

HOW MUCH SLEEP DO YOU NEED?

Studies have shown that teens aged 13-18 need somewhere between 8 and 10 hours of sleep every night, preferably on a regular schedule. This means going to bed and getting up at approximately the same time each day – yes, including on weekends!

Building a regular sleeping routine trains your brain to know when it should be alert, and when it is "on a break." If you have a somewhat regular bedtime, you might notice that when you stay up later than usual you start to get tired around the time you usually fall asleep. This is not only because you've been up for more hours than usual, it is also a natural reaction of your brain, which has been trained to think that this is the correct time to go to sleep. Your brain begins to wire down and you become groggy and unfocused. When you do not have a regular routine, it's difficult to train your brain in this way – and you risk being on high alert for many hours in a row because you are not giving your brain and body the time they need to regroup and gather their energy.

BEDTIME HABITS

- Comfort is a huge factor in the quality of your sleep. Investing in a good mattress and comfortable pillows can make a huge change to how rested you feel when you wake up in the morning. There is nothing worse than waking up after a few hours of sleep and feeling unrested.

- Avoid eating heavy food and ingesting caffeine for three hours before you go to sleep. When you sleep, your digestive system slows down with you. If you eat too close to bedtime, your body doesn't have enough time to properly digest your food and that can cause indigestion or discomfort. Caffeine, which can be found in coffee, some teas, soft drinks, and more, is a stimulant. Essentially, it makes your brain stay awake and alert which can be good during the day – but disastrous at night.

- Spend around half an hour before you go to sleep winding down. Evolution has taught us that when it is dark outside, it is time to sleep. Bright lights from screens and other electronics can trick the primitive part of our mind into thinking it is still daytime – leading to high alert and restlessness, and preventing your brain from slowing down as it should. Instead, before falling asleep you can read a book, meditate, write in your journal, or just reflect on your day.

- Be active. Staying active during the day is great for our health and also beneficial to effective sleep. Think about it as tiring out your body and brain just the right amount so that you can start fresh and new the next day – after a good night's sleep.

CHAPTER 17:

WARDROBE ESSENTIALS

Whether you're at school, going out with friends, running errands, or interviewing for a job, being mindful of how you look and dress is a big part of the impression you make on others.

It's easy sometimes to fall back on the same boring outfits day in and day out, especially on a busy schedule when you don't have much time to spend in front of your wardrobe. The trick to easily put together an outfit for any occasion is building a basis of essential pieces of clothing, which you can mix and match and add to as needed.

These are some must-haves for every teen boy's closet:

BASIC BLACK AND WHITE T-SHIRTS

These are excellent base pieces for any outfit. You can dress them up with fitted pants and a blazer, or down with jeans and a jacket – the plain tee is a versatile piece of clothing to invest in.

HIGH-QUALITY JEANS

Jeans, though on the casual side, are essential for any teen boy. Make sure the fit and length are right for you and that they are comfortable enough to spend a day in. Great for school, errands, going out, or staying in – a good pair of jeans is a must.

A JACKET

Whether denim, leather, or bomber, a jacket is essential for those in-between-season days. They are a light solution to cooler weather and easy to layer over and match with almost any outfit.

SNEAKERS

Comfortable, durable, and stylish, simple sneakers can add a finishing touch to a variety of outfits and are a convenient way to look good while feeling great.

A SUIT AND TIE

When you need to keep things formal for a job interview, wedding, party, or another classy event, you can't go wrong with a suit and tie. Have at least one suit in a neutral color (black, navy blue, or gray) in your wardrobe and a tie to match.

Here are some basic guidelines for putting together an outfit that matches:

- Choose one piece that is your statement piece and work around it – it can be a top, pants, shoes, accessory, or anything. Set up the rest of your outfit with more muted garments to make your statement piece pop.

- Experiment with layers – layering can give a look more depth, so try putting a button-down under a sweater or adding a blazer to a sweater.

- Know which colors match – avoid pairing black with other dark colors like brown or navy, or bright colors with other bright colors. Make sure to have some neutral-colored pieces to combine with brighter ones.

PART 4:
MONEY AND BUDGETING

CHAPTER 18:
PLANNING A BUDGET

Learning how to make a budget and stick to it is a great skill to master when preparing for adulthood. Being financially responsible and knowing how to manage your expenses will make adulting that much easier once you're living away from home, and supporting yourself.

The first, and most important thing, is to figure out your income and expenses.

INCOME is all the money that you acquire or earn – from work, allowance, gifts, etc.

EXPENSES refer to the total sum of money you spend in a given time.

It's common to look at income and expenses on a monthly or weekly basis, so start by figuring out your average monthly or weekly cash flow – whichever you prefer.

You can divide each into categories, putting together a table that looks something like this, but customized to your own needs:

INCOME (MONTHLY)

CATEGORY	AMOUNT ($)
Allowance	
Work	

Gifts	
Other	
TOTAL	

EXPENSES (WEEKLY)

CATEGORY	AMOUNT ($)
Gas	
Entertainment	
Beauty and grooming	
Other	
TOTAL	

Once you've filled out the tables, subtract your total expenses from your total income. If you're left with a positive value, that means your expenses do not exceed your income and you are managing to save some money. If the value is negative, that means you're overspending your income.

Tracking your habits like this, on a weekly or monthly basis, is the first step to becoming financially conscious. When you are intentional about how much you make and spend, you can be responsible with your money and know where you should be cutting down your spending and by how much.

After figuring out your total monthly spending pattern, you can take measures to reduce expenses in the next months.

Budgeting means deciding in advance how much you are willing or able to spend on certain expenses while taking into account the income you receive.

Your expenses can be categorized into three types: **NECESSARY**, **EXTRAS**, and **SAVINGS**.

Your necessary expenses are the ones that you cannot avoid – gas, groceries, tuition, etc.

Extras are luxuries you allow yourself (which are important as well) – eating out, entertainment, travel, shopping, etc.

Savings refers to the money you put away, not to be used. You can learn more about saving money in the next chapter.

To set your budgeting goals, outline a realistic monthly or weekly budget for each type of expense in the "extras" category, as these are the ones you have control over.

You may decide to cut down on takeaway meals, or bike to school instead of taking public transport. You might limit yourself to a certain amount of money you can spend on clothes each month, or opt for cheaper options when choosing where to eat.

THIS PART IS UP TO YOU – BUT REMEMBER THESE IMPORTANT GUIDELINES:

- Try to budget in a way that will balance your income and expenses so that you are not overspending.

- Once you've decided on a budget you'll have to stick to it. So make your plans realistic and achievable.

- Consider ways to increase your income if you see that it is not enough to cover your expenses – you can find odd jobs like babysitting or tutoring, or get a steady job you can commit to over time.

CHAPTER 19:

SAVING UP

Having a budget and sticking to it is great preparation for adult life, and a first step toward financial stability. But if you feel ready to take your finances one step further and also secure some funds for your future, you need to understand the basics of saving.

You might want to start saving up for your college tuition, your first car, or simply put away some money for anything you may one day need. Either way, you'll find that money gets spent easily, without you even noticing, when it is there in your wallet or sitting in your bank account.

The idea behind saving is putting a certain sum of money away where it is not as readily available to spend and letting that money accumulate over time. Developing good savings habits as a teenager, when you don't yet have many financial obligations, can be a life-changing skill!

To start saving, you'll need three things:

1. A job or other steady income
2. Somewhere to put the money – in a physical place or a savngs account in the bank
2. A plan

DECIDE WHERE YOUR MONEY WILL BE........

Most banks offer teenagers savings accounts without a monthly fee. Ask your parents which bank services they use or research local banks and their benefits. Some savings accounts also offer interest, which means that the money you have in the account will earn interest at a certain rate determined by the bank, according to the deposited sum and how well you can negotiate your terms.

Alternatively, if you're saving for a more immediate goal and you receive your allowance or salary in cash, you may just want to put some money aside in a safe place at home until you have enough to spend.

INCREASE YOUR INCOME AND DECREASE YOUR SPENDING

Even if your parents give you an allowance or if you're earning money from odd jobs or a regular gig, there are always ways to increase your income. The more you earn – the more you can save! You can pick up a summer job, create things and sell them, or utilize your skills to secure some freelance work.

Another way to save money is to decrease your spending. You can refer back to chapter 18, *Planning a Budget*, for ways of being more frugal with your finances.

SET A GOAL AND MAKE A PLAN

Your goal can be specific – for example, you want to save enough money for a big trip after graduation. In this case, your goal will have a desired sum and a deadline. Your goal can also be general – save X amount of money every month, or Y percent of your income every month. Either way, having a goal in mind will keep you motivated to stick to your savings plan.

Saving money has to be a deliberate effort. Make a systematic plan that fits your income and is realistic with regard to your goals. Consider your regular expenses and don't overestimate how much you can reasonably save, because you don't want to find yourself in a situation where you are unable to meet your weekly or monthly goal. Calculate your income and expenses and see how much there is left to put away.

Once you have a specific number in mind, break down your goal and turn it into a habit. It can be daily, weekly, or monthly, or it can even be automated if you're working with a bank account, but it should be something that is cemented into your financial mindset and considered just another one of your necessary expenses – that way, you'll be more likely to stick to your goal.

CHAPTER 20:

TAXES

Taxes are fees that we, as law-abiding citizens, pay to the state or government. In return, these payments are invested in institutes and projects that benefit the general population, such as building roads, parks, schools, and recreational centers or funding public healthcare, social security, and national defense.

There are all sorts of different taxes, none of which children have to pay. But as a teenager, as you grow older and more financially responsible, you will need to know the meaning of taxation, the different kinds of tax you will be subjected to, and how to pay them.

INCOME TAX

Anyone who works and earns an income has to allocate some of that income to tax. That means you as well, once you join the workforce.

All US citizens are required to file tax returns every year. The more you earn, the more tax you pay – as the tax is calculated by percentage of income.

In the UK, most people pay their taxes "at source" – which means that their tax is automatically deducted from their paycheck if they are employed. Therefore, UK citizens don't have to file their tax returns themselves, unless they are self-employed.

You can learn more about income tax in chapter 35, *Understanding Your Paycheck*!

SALES TAX

This is a tax that you pay on any purchase you make – from purchases as small as a soda to ones as big as a car. When you pay for something in a store, the sum written on the label usually already includes a certain percentage of sales tax, which you pay automatically without even realizing it.

You can usually look at the receipt for an item or service to see just how much of the sum you paid was the actual cost of the purchase, and how much was added due to tax.

Each state and country can determine for itself the percentage of sales tax it charges its citizens.

Some products are exempt from sales tax, such as fundamental groceries (like fruit and vegetables) and certain prescription medicines.

PROPERTY TAX

As a teenager, it's likely that you don't yet own a property – such as a house or apartment. But your parents or someone else you know might, and you may own property yourself someday.

Anyone who owns a property of any size must pay the government a tax based on the property's value. There are professionals who know how to assess a property's value, and they in turn calculate how much a house, apartment, building, or agricultural space is worth and how much its owner needs to pay in return for it belonging to them.

Paying taxes for hard work you've done or purchases you've worked to save up for might seem unfair – but remember that the taxes we pay, in the end, come back to benefit us and our friends and families. They are also a way to ensure that people who are less fortunate than we are, have the resources to lead a comfortable, healthy life.

CHAPTER 21:

CREDIT SCORE

You may have heard people or advertisements saying things about having a "good" or "bad" credit score. But first things first, what is a credit score anyway? Let's start by understanding the idea of paying with credit.

In the past, making financial transactions was a simple thing. If you have the money you needed to purchase something, you could hand it over and it would be rightfully yours.

In the 20th century, the concept of paying with credit emerged. Paying with credit is a sort of promise that even though you don't have the cash on you right now, you can ensure that you will be able to pay for the goods or services later. Credit cards are the best example of this – your credit card is connected to your bank account and you can use it to buy things that you will pay for at the end of the month, or even over the course of several months or years.

A credit score is a number on a scale of 300-850, which determines your financial credibility. It lets banks, landlords, and some businesses know how financially stable you are and how likely you are to be able to uphold your promise of paying them later.

The higher your credit score is, the better – so a score above 800 is considered excellent, anything over 650 is considered good, and any score under that is perceived as only "fair" or even "poor."

HOW IS A CREDIT SCORE DETERMINED?

There are all sorts of things that can affect your credit score.

1. **DEBT.** When you overspend your income regularly or owe money to someone, it can lower your credit score because it indicates that you may not be financially responsible or earn enough income to be a trustworthy buyer. This is why it is important to budget carefully and avoid spending more than you can afford, which you can learn more about if you jump back a few pages to chapter 18, *Planning a Budget*.

2. **PAYMENT HISTORY.** A big part of your credit score is determined by how promptly you make your payments. If you have a history of late payments for bills, utilities, or credit cards, you run the risk of hurting your score. So make sure to always be prompt and responsible with your bills once you have them!

3. **CREDIT HISTORY LENGTH.** The longer you've held a credit account, the higher your score will be. This might be bad news for young adults just starting out, but it only affects approximately 15% of your score – so no need to worry about that yet!

WHY IS HAVING A GOOD CREDIT SCORE IMPORTANT?

When you're just starting out in life as a teenager with your first bank account, there's no reason why you shouldn't have an excellent credit score. Maintaining a good credit score is important because it affects the financial opportunities you will be able to have in the future.

When you leave home and want to rent your first apartment, your landlord can look at your credit score to help him decide if you will be a good tenant, or if he should go with someone else with a better credit score.

Also, when you apply for a job, employers have the right to include your credit score in the various considerations they take into account when deciding whether or not to hire you.

Equally importantly, if at some point in your life, you want to take out a loan from the bank, the bank can refuse to loan you money, or limit the amount of money you can borrow, if they see that you have a history of low credit.

TIPS FOR MAINTAINING AN EXCELLENT CREDIT SCORE

- Stick to a realistic budget that does not exceed your income.
- Use as few credit cards as possible – preferably just one, especially when you're young.
- Always pay your bills on time.
- Try not to max out on your monthly credit account.
- Put money aside in a savings account for emergencies.

PART 5:

SOCIAL SKILLS

CHAPTER 22:

EMERGENCY CONTACTS

Knowing how to act in an emergency is an important skill to learn. It is always better to be safe than sorry, so having a list of emergency contacts ready and knowing whom to call in what situation can make all the difference if you ever find yourself or someone else in need of urgent help.

Here is a list of contacts you should write down or save in your phone for emergencies:

- **911** (112 in Europe, or your country's equivalent) – dialing this number will direct you to an operator with the resources to dispatch any help you may need. This number is only to be dialed in emergencies – including immediate medical risk, life-threatening situations, crimes in progress, fires, car accidents, or any situation where you feel that you or someone else is in immediate danger. It is essential to provide the operator with as much information as possible so that they can dispatch the appropriate response – police, firefighting, or medical services.

- **YOUR PARENTS OR CARETAKER** – have these numbers easily accessible, and preferably know them off by heart, to quickly dial or dictate to others in emergencies.

- **POISON CONTROL** – numbers may differ according to your region. Call poison control when you know or suspect that someone has or may have come into contact with any form of poison – this includes overdosing on medication and venomous bites or stings, as well as ingesting poisonous substances.

- **LOCAL POLICE STATION AND LOCAL FIRE DEPARTMENT** – while during an emergency it is always to best to dial 911 or its equivalent, save these numbers to use when you need general help or information that is not immediate.

- **VETERINARIAN** – whether you have a pet or not, having your local veterinarian's number on hand is useful for helping animals who are lost, injured, or require other medical assistance.

- **MENTAL HEALTH SERVICE** – depending on where you are, there are local or national hotlines you can call when you feel you are in need of immediate mental health or emotional support. These hotlines can direct you to someone you can talk to, or in case of emergency dispatch appropriate help. Make sure to locate and have a number available in case you or anyone you know ever needs help.

CHAPTER 23:

BASIC ETIQUETTE

"Etiquette" is a set of unspoken rules or customs accepted in a certain society. Etiquette can vary according to your culture or geographical location and has certainly changed over time. Being aware of the basic rules of etiquette helps us function in society – it makes us pleasant to be around and shows that we care about how we look and sound and that we have good manners.

SOCIALIZING

Different social situations call for different etiquette. When you're hanging out with your friends in a casual setting, you can behave casually. If, however, the setting is more formal, you'll want to use less slang, be more mindful of how you speak, and act according to the situation.

When you're invited over to someone's house or to an event, it is customary to bring a small thank-you gift to show gratitude for the invitation. Similarly, if someone gives you a gift, make sure to keep a note of it so that you can thank them later for being so considerate, and even let them know that you are enjoying it. For example, if your aunt gives you a book as a birthday gift, you can send her a message to let her know you've finished the book and what you thought about it. This not only shows that you are a considerate person, but it makes people feel special and appreciated.

DINING OUT

When eating out at a restaurant, café, or other venue, be sure to be polite to your server.

Jobs in the service industry are often held by teenagers just like you who are working hard to make money and probably saving up for college or other expenses. Even if service is slow or your order is not delivered perfectly, be courteous to your server and remember – it isn't even necessarily their fault.

Wait for everyone to get their food before you start eating. Eating alone or before everyone else is ready can make for awkward or uncomfortable situations.

Tipping is customary in most establishments. If you are not satisfied with your service, you can express your dissatisfaction by leaving a review or contacting the business later. Never take out your frustration directly on a server or employee, and avoid withholding tips when you can. Remember, many teenagers in these jobs earn fairly low salaries and often rely on tips to supplement their income!

GOOD HYGIENE AND DRESSING RIGHT

In chapter 15, *Personal Hygiene*, we went over how to keep your skin, hair, teeth, and body healthy and clean. Later, in chapter 17, *Wardrobe Essentials*, we talked about how to put together outfits and to look respectable.

How you look, sound and even smell can have a big impact on how you are perceived by others and are a big part of the unspoken language of etiquette.

HERE ARE SOME GOOD MANNERS TO PRACTICE WHEN OUT IN PUBLIC:

- Make and maintain eye contact when someone is speaking to you.

- Avoid walking around with your eyes glued to a screen, especially in social settings.

- Don't chew gum when you're talking to someone.

- Dress for the occasion – consider where you're going and choose an appropriate outfit.

- Look yourself over before you go out to check for creased or dirty clothes, untidy hair, or food between your teeth.

- Express gratitude regularly – to the bus driver who got you to your destination, the store clerk who rang up your purchase, and your parents or friends who gave you a ride or did you a favor.

CHAPTER 24:

NAVIGATING SOCIAL MEDIA

One of the most prominent characteristics of the 21st century is globalization and, with it, the rise of social media. Much of our communication is held through screens and online, and much of our time is occupied with various apps and media platforms.

Social media can be a wonderful thing – it can inspire, connect, teach, and bring people together. However, it is also something to be wary of, and learning to use it right is a crucial skill for the modern teen.

The most important thing to keep in mind when you decide to engage with this content is that there is a strong element of choice in what people present to the world. Some accounts may be more candid than others, and certainly, many people choose to use their social media personas to provide a refreshing and authentic experience for viewers. But even then, the act of creating social content is thought out and calculated. Remember, social media is not a mirror of real life.

Here are some things to look out for when engaging with social content:

ONLINE SAFETY AND PRIVACY

It is easy to unintentionally share private or personal information online. Be mindful of this, and make sure never to share your personal address or information with people you do not know and trust, or on a public platform.

Be wary of other users reaching out through comments or private messages, particularly if they are asking for information or encouraging you to meet with them. If something doesn't feel right to you – trust your instincts!

Most platforms allow you to change the privacy settings to help you control who sees your information, photos, and videos. Consult with your parents or a trusted adult on how to manage your privacy settings.

Similarly, remember that other people's private information is not yours to share – respect others' privacy like you would want them to respect yours.

CYBERBULLYING

People express themselves more freely – positively and negatively – from behind the protection of a screen. This makes it easier to make hurtful or insulting comments without having to face social consequences.

If you see something like this, targeting you or anyone else, you can report the user. Don't hesitate to block or unfollow content that makes you feel uncomfortable or upset.

Be conscious of the power you wield on your social media accounts as well – always think before you comment or post and be considerate of other people's feelings.

MENTAL HEALTH

With all the wonderful benefits of social media, we can sometimes not realize how it's affecting our mental health. Spending too much time in the magical world of TikTok or Instagram can be dangerously time-consuming, and even has the power to affect your self-confidence, happiness, and productivity.

Try to limit the amount of time you spend online – and designate times and places which are strictly social media-free. This could be mealtimes, family time, evenings before you go to sleep, outings with friends, time designated for studying, or any other setting you deem appropriate.

CHAPTER 25:
RESOLVING CONFLICT

Conflict is something human beings face all the time in life – with our parents, siblings, friends, teacher, co-workers, and strangers on the street. Some people are more avoidant of conflict and it causes them extreme discomfort, while others are less bothered and more eager to participate in a heated debate or argument.

Conflict in itself is not a bad thing – disagreements and arguments can often lead to growth and improvement when they are conducted maturely and respectfully. But what happens when conflict escalates? How can you resolve or reduce conflict without leading to insult, anger, or a physical altercation?

First, let's pin down the different types of strategies people use when they find themselves in conflict.

The Thomas-Kilman model lays out five different conflict management strategies, which are determined by two axes – assertiveness (or, how important it is to achieve your goal) and cooperativeness (or, how important your relationship with the other person is):

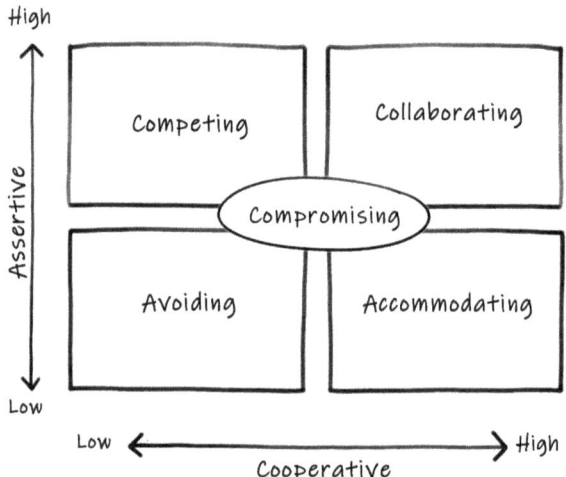

AVOIDING

When your motivation to achieve your goal is low, as is the importance of your relationship with the other person, the classic strategy is avoidance. Avoidance doesn't solve anything, but then again, the problem probably isn't important enough to solve.

COMPETING

Competing is an uncooperative strategy that relies on one person "winning" the argument and another one "losing." This usually happens in a conflict between two people who don't much care for each other over something very important to both.

ACCOMMODATING

In this method, where the relationship is more important to one or both sides than the goal, one side will agree to accommodate the other by compromising on their own wants or needs to fulfill the other's. This is a good short-term solution for resolving an argument without causing harm to a friendship.

COLLABORATING

This is the highest level of conflict resolution – both parties work together to find a solution that benefits both of them equally. Successful collaboration is a win-win situation!

COMPROMISING

In a sort of lose-lose solution, both sides compromise on their goals in the interest of reaching an agreement.

Now that we better understand the different types of conflicts, there are several important steps you can take to resolve disagreements, whether you're involved in them or a witness to them.

1. First, understand the source of the conflict. What is the problem? Think about each side and what they might be frustrated or angry about.

2. Next, allow each side to express their opinions and feelings. This important step can go a long way to calm the atmosphere – simply allowing people to get things off their chest can lower frustration levels.

3. Work hard to come up with a solution that is as close to win-win as possible. It's likely you won't come up with a solution that everyone's completely happy with, otherwise, there wouldn't have been an argument in the first place. Make sure both sides' needs are met equally, and decide on the most mutually beneficial resolution.

Knowing how to approach and resolve conflict is a way to strengthen your relationships with those around you and improve your confidence, self-worth, and emotional intelligence.

CHAPTER 26:

HAVING DIFFICULT CONVERSATIONS

Have you ever had that uneasy feeling in your belly when you knew you had to talk to someone about something, but you were dreading it?

It could be when you were called into the principal's office one day at school, or when one of your parents asked to speak with you after you did something you knew was wrong. Perhaps you needed to tell someone close to you something that you knew they wouldn't take well – maybe it was a breakup conversation or a conversation about values with someone who thinks differently from you.

Communication is something that we engage in constantly, even without noticing. It is how we relate to other people, express our wants and needs, it is how we build relationships and make things happen. Most of the time, communication is effortless and comes naturally to us, we don't even have to think about it. But, sometimes we find ourselves in a position where we are required or expected to partake in a conversation that makes us feel uncomfortable, or even scared.

These kinds of conversations usually pertain to something that is not trivial – they will focus on an issue that is of significant importance either to you or to the person you're having the conversation with, which is why they can feel more charged and meaningful than a regular discussion. This is also why you might be avoidant of such a conversation.

The thing about these situations is that in the end, the conversation is going to have to happen. You can either do it on your own terms and time, or wait it out until tensions rise and it becomes unavoidable. The first option is usually more sensible and leads to more effective communication.

SO FIRST, TAKE A DEEP BREATH. THEN, FOLLOW THESE STEPS:

1. Before you start, organize your thoughts. Think through what it is you have to say, even practice in your head a few times, that way it'll be easier to get the words out in the moment of truth.

2. Be open to listening. The person on the other side of the conflict is likely feeling as uncomfortable as you are. Allow them to have their say and express their thoughts and emotions just as you expect to communicate your own. By listening attentively, you may learn something you didn't know that can change how you look at the entire situation.

3. Try not to make it personal. One of the reasons some people tend to avoid conflict or difficult conversations is that they are worried about not being liked. When you look at the bigger picture and address the issue without using insults or accusations, you're more likely to be able to conduct a mature discussion.

4. Realize that you don't have to agree in the end. Not every conversation is meant to convince, and there isn't always one person who's right and another who's wrong. Sometimes, it helps just to talk. Even if you don't solve the problem, talking and listening can help you reconnect, which is sometimes all you need.

In the end, what you have to keep in mind is that as anxious as you may be about the conversation you know you need to have, you can almost always be sure that you will feel better after you've had it.

PART 6:

PERSONAL DEVELOPMENT

CHAPTER 27:

TIME MANAGEMENT

School, hobbies, work, friends, and extracurricular activities can make for a busy, and sometimes even stressful, timetable. There's so much to do and so few hours in the day to do it in, and it's easy to feel overwhelmed. That's where managing your time efficiently and effectively comes in.

Time management is the skill of planning and prioritizing, and when mastered, it can make a real difference in your life.

MAKE A LIST

First things first – get everything down on paper or in a digital file. When our brain is too full, we're bound to forget something! So keeping a running list, or making a new one every day, week, or even month, will help keep your time in order. You can organize your tasks by type, and even put in things that aren't necessarily "tasks", but that you'd like to make time for – like hobbies, exercising, meeting with friends, etc.

PRIORITIZE

Once you've got a list of the things you need to do, the Eisenhower Matrix can be an extremely useful tool when deciding which ones to do first.

IT WORKS LIKE THIS:

Each task can be ranked on two scales – urgency and importance. For each thing on your list, decide whether it is urgent or not, and whether it is important or not. Remember – important is not necessarily objective! Something that someone else might rank as unimportant could be important to you.

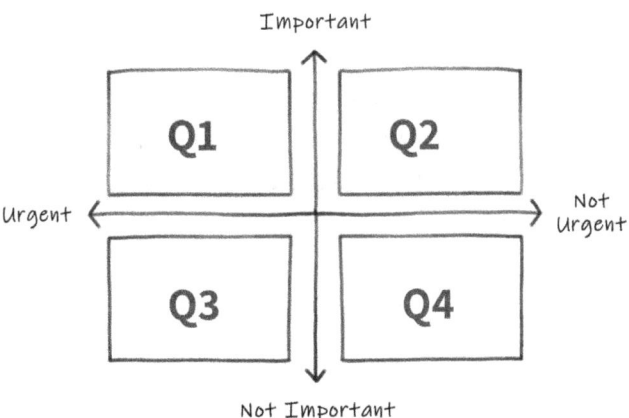

For example, a school paper that is due tomorrow is urgent and important, so that will go in Quadrant 1.

Going out to buy a gift for a friend whose birthday is in a week is important, but not urgent – put it in Quadrant 2.

The numbering of the quadrants tells you exactly how to prioritize your tasks. Start with Quadrant 1, urgent and important – do these things as soon as possible. Then, go on to Quadrant 2, important but not urgent. This might include exercising, reading, meditating, or anything else that is important to you but not time-sensitive. Fit these into your schedule whenever you have time to spare. Quadrant 3, not important but urgent, are things that you may be able to delegate to others. If not, schedule these for specific times, according to their deadline. Anything that goes into the final quadrant, not urgent and not important, should be crossed off your list. If it's not time-sensitive and it's not important to you, just don't do it – save your time for other more relevant tasks.

KEEP A SCHEDULE

Keeping a schedule is a good way to make sure your time is managed efficiently and no important things slip your mind. Use a calendar or a time-management app to monitor your tasks and prioritize like a pro.

CHAPTER 28:

SETTING PERSONAL GOALS

From childhood all the way to adulthood, we have hopes and dreams. When we're younger, our goals are simpler and smaller – getting to eat what we want for dinner, buying a toy we want, or reading a certain book. As you grow older, your goals can become bigger and more long-term – getting into that sports team you've been training for, landing a college scholarship, starting a business, or finding a relationship.

Big dreams can be hard to conceptualize – and may be daunting when not broken down into smaller, more obtainable goals. For example, if your goal is to improve your chances of getting accepted into the college of your choice by the end of the school year, that big goal can be partitioned into smaller goals that are within your reach. You can set a goal to improve in one specific subject by Christmas, decide to take private lessons in another, and earn extra credit by joining a sports team or club.

Research shows that when faced with only one big task, people are less likely to complete it and more likely to despair than if faced with several, more accomplishable targets.

In addition, if your goals are too vague or general, even with the best of intentions, you might find yourself lost on the way to accomplishing them.

HERE ARE THE THREE TRICKS TO EFFECTIVE GOAL-SETTING:

1. Have a clear, well-defined target.
2. Break that target down into smaller goals.
3. Make a plan and stick to it.

Effective goal-setting is an important skill, and one that encompasses in it other skills as well – such as time management, self-discipline, organization, and budgeting. You can read more about how to budget properly in chapter 18, *Planning a Budget*, and about managing your time in chapter 27, *Time Management*.

SET YOUR GOALS

It is important to be mindful and intentional about our goals. People need dreams and aspirations to keep them going, and accomplishments, however big or small, are part of what gives us purpose and satisfaction in life. That's part of the reason why people make New Year's resolutions – we all want to be better, happier, more successful, or more content with our lives. However, experience shows that the vast majority of these resolutions are not destined to last. The main reasons for people *not* sticking to their New Year's resolutions are that they set big, often unrealistic goals, don't know how to section them into achievable objectives, and don't take the time to make a detailed plan of action.

Write down your end goals in the exercise sheet at the end of this chapter. You can have one or many, they can be academic, social, financial, or personal, as long as they are authentic and realistic. Try to define them in more than one word or two. For example, a goal that might have looked like this in your head: "have more money" should look more like this on the page: "earn a steady monthly income that surpasses my expenses by 10%", or "earn X sum of money by next January so that I can purchase my first car."

BREAK DOWN YOUR GOALS INTO SUB-GOALS . .

Next, try and analyze each goal you've written down and section it into smaller objectives. These are your sub-goals, which will help you on your way to your end goal. These targets should be feasible, simple, and limited by time. Following our previous example: "find a part-time job with a salary of $X per hour by the end of the month," "open a savings account and deposit X amount of money each month," "have a yard sale to earn money from all the things I don't use anymore but are in good condition within the next six months," etc., etc.

Finally, translate your sub-goals into actionable tasks and put them in a calendar. Give each task a target date that is realistic with your end goal and have your plan in a prominent place where you can look at it often. Forgotten dreams will never be realized, so having your goals at the front of your mind always will ensure that you are mindful about working towards them every day!

MY GOALS AND SUB-GOALS:

1. ....
   a. ....
   b. ....
   c. ....
   d. ....
   e. ....

2. ....
   a. ....
   b. ....
   c. ....
   d. ....
   e. ....

3. ....
   a. ....
   b. ....
   c. ....
   d. ....
   e. ....

CHAPTER 29:

CAR CARE AND MAINTENANCE

As a teen, you probably can't wait to pass your driver's test, or you've recently acquired your license. Having a driver's license is a huge leap into adulthood – it's a new freedom to get yourself where you need to go without relying on an adult to take you there, as long as there is a vehicle available for you to use.

But being a driver is more than just getting from A to B. Cars are complicated machines that need regular care and maintenance to run as they were designed to, and taking on the freedom of driving means also taking on the responsibility of maintaining your vehicle.

Whether you have your own car or plan to drive your parents' or a rental, there are important things you should know about how to properly care for it.

GETTING GAS

Most cars run on gas. This means that once in a while, depending on how often and how far you drive, you will need to get to a gas station to pump gas. There is a dial on the dashboard that should tell you how much gas is left in the tank, and a red light that will flick on when you're low. Don't let the gas tank empty out completely, as this can be bad for the car and also puts you at risk of finding yourself stuck on the road.

When you get to the gas station, locate your gas tank. Some cars have a lever by the driver's seat that opens the tank, while others simply have a handle on the side of the car. Open up and unscrew the plastic cover.

Next, think about the grade of gas you need. There are different types of gas – regular, mid-grade, and premium. Choose the correct one as detailed in your car's user manual.

Lastly, pay for the gas and fit the nozzle in the gas tank to fill it up. In some gas stations you will be able to pay with credit, in others you may have to walk inside to pay with cash.

Don't forget to screw the cover back on once you're finished!

TIRE PRESSURE

Each car has a recommended tire pressure. Driving with under-or-overinflated tires is not ideal and should be avoided whenever possible. You can use a simple pressure device to check the pressure yourself, and if you find that it is too high or too low, make your way to the nearest gas station ASAP where you can pump air into the tires.

If you see that your tire has gone flat and remains flat even after you've filled it with air, you may have a flat tire. Get someone to help you change the tire or drive carefully to a car service.

CHANGING OIL

Oil changes are just as important as keeping your tires inflated. The oil in your car keeps the engine lubricated and running smoothly. Every so often, when you're parked on level ground and the engine has cooled, check the oil levels by popping the hood and finding the oil "dipstick" – a long contraption with a bright handle that is inserted into the engine. Pull the dipstick out and clean it with a rag or cloth. Then, insert it back in and pull it out once it hits the bottom. You will be able to see how high the oil levels are by the oil that has stayed on the stick. If the markings on the dipstick indicate that the oil is low, that means it's time to get to a car service and have it changed.

PREPARING FOR AN EMERGENCY . . . .

Staying on top of your car's maintenance will minimize the chances of your car causing you trouble and possibly malfunctioning on the road.

Pay attention to any warning lights that may appear on the dashboard and deal with them without delay. If your "check engine" light is on, make a beeline to the closest car repair shop to have it looked at.

Here are some of the warning lights you may see on your dashboard and what they all mean:

 Check oil

 Check tire pressure

 Engine overheating

 Problem with the Anti-Lock Braking System, which prevents your wheels from locking up on slick surfaces

 Check engine

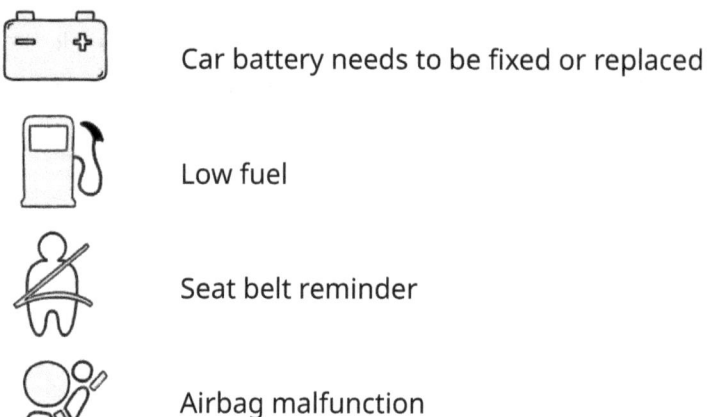

Car battery needs to be fixed or replaced

Low fuel

Seat belt reminder

Airbag malfunction

Whenever you're unsure of something, refer to the car's user manual which should be in the vehicle at all times!

ELECTRIC CARS

While most vehicles still run on gas, electric cars are quickly growing more popular around the world. On the one hand, electric cars are incredibly energy-efficient and are better for the environment because they create less emissions. They also need far less maintenance than gas vehicles. On the other hand, they are limited in how far they can travel before they need to be recharged, and at least for now, they are significantly more expensive than their gas counterparts.

CHAPTER 30:
BASICS OF CAMPING

Camping is an excellent way to get out of the house, connect with nature, bond with friends and family, and hone your survival skills. It can be tricky to plan a camping trick on your own, but with a few tips and tricks, you'll be ready to embark on a camping adventure in no time.

GEAR

When going out into the wilderness overnight (or a campsite, which is slightly more organized than wilderness but still outdoors), you'll need to take some essentials with you.

- **A TENT** – tents come in different sizes and shapes, so choose the one that is best suited to your needs. Some take more of an effort to put up while others pop right up at the push of a button or the pull of a string. If you plan to take a lot of equipment with you, pack a tent that is larger than you need so that you can fit everything inside.

- **SOMETHING TO SLEEP ON** – depending on just how much you intend to rough it, you'll want to pack an air mattress, a sleeping pad, or a simple blanket. Sleeping directly on the ground can be uncomfortable and can ruin the experience, so take this into account when packing your camping gear.

- **LIGHTING** – a handheld flashlight or battery-powered lantern is essential when you're camping out in the wilderness.

It gets very dark out at night when you're away from big cities or towns, and you don't want to find yourself completely in the dark.

- **COOKING EQUIPMENT AND FOOD** – if your camping trip is short you can bring ready-made meals with you from home, but for longer trips, it's best to have some supplies and equipment to cook them with. Check in advance to make sure that your campsite allows campfires if that is part of your plan.

- **TOILETRIES** – it's likely that wherever you camp you will not have access to clean toiletries like toilet paper, toothpaste, and soap, so pack those with you.

- **EXTRAS** – if you're camping in a group you can bring along some games or activities to play together, books to read, or a loudspeaker to play music on (just make sure not to disturb other campers or wildlife). You can pack some fairy lights to give your campsite a magical look or add some comfy cushions to sit on around the campfire.

PREPARATIONS

Besides packing all of your equipment and gear, here are some things you can do in advance to make your camping trip easier, safer, and more enjoyable:

- **RESEARCH CAMPSITES** – choose the best campsite depending on whether you're camping alone, with friends, or with family, and whether or not children are involved. Some campgrounds offer facilities, electricity, and even equipment, and others offer nothing but a space to pitch your tent and get in touch with nature. Check which campsites allow fires, how far they are from home, whether pets are allowed, etc.

- **PRACTICE PITCHING YOUR TENT** – pitching a tent can be tough, especially once you're already out in nature, so take some time to practice once or twice in the backyard or at home before you leave.

- **PLAN YOUR MEALS** – figure out how long you'll be away from home and how many people are coming, to calculate how much food you will need. Then, decide which food and snacks you will prepare at home, what you will need to buy on the way, and what and how you will be cooking at the campsite.

Camping can be an exciting, refreshing, and memorable experience – follow these tips and your next trip is sure to be a success!

CHAPTER 31:

GRILLING

Food brings people together. And what better way to celebrate a social gathering than with a hot, hearty grilled meal?

Grilling is an incredibly versatile cooking medium. If you know how to use one, it can be so much more than just steaks and burgers on the 4th of July – and the whole atmosphere of having a barbecue outside in the fresh air makes for an enjoyable experience for everyone.

To become an expert griller, you must first understand the difference between different types of grills: electric, gas, or charcoal.

CHARCOAL GRILL

This is the simplest version, usually just a hollow drum or rectangle made of metal with a metal grate on top. Charcoal grills use coals to heat food and are usually portable, so they can be taken with you on camping trips or picnics. They are cheaper than electric and gas grills, but more difficult to use.

GAS GRILL

Gas grills are stationary – they sit in the garden or on a balcony and you can't take them camping with you. They run on gas, just like a gas stovetop, and connect to your home's gas supply. These grills have knobs and buttons to help control the heat of the flames while cooking.

ELECTRIC GRILL

An electric grill connects to an outlet and uses electrical current to heat food. They vary in size and the smaller ones can be portable, and even used inside the kitchen, as they do not produce too much smoke.

SETTING UP YOUR GRILL

No matter which type of grill you have, you need to prep it before you can use it. First, ensure that it is clean. You can use a steel brush to clean the metal grate and remove any food residue from your last cookout. Next, clean out the surface of the grill, beneath the grate.

Grilling directly on a dry grate can cause your food to stick, so apply a thin, even layer of vegetable oil to the metal while the grill is still cold.

Next, turn on the heat. With gas and electric grills, all you have to do is use the buttons or dials to set the heat to the right temperature.

IF YOU'RE USING A CHARCOAL GRILL, FOLLOW THESE SIMPLE STEPS:

1. Arrange the charcoal in a pile at the base of your grill (at this point, the metal grate should not be on the grill).

2. Carefully add some lighter fluid or charcoal starter.

3. Light the charcoal with a match, making sure it catches in two or three places.

4   Wait for the coals to heat and turn white and the flames to go down, then (carefully!) use tongs or a stick to collapse the pile and distribute the charcoal evenly over the surface.

5   Wearing gloves to protect your hands from the heat, place the grate on top of the grill, over the coals. You're ready to start grilling!

TURNING A SIMPLE GRILL INTO A MEAL . . . .

Now that you know how to use your grill, let's figure out what you can put on it to produce a meal for friends, family, or just yourself.

Proteins like steak, chicken breast, hot dogs, kebabs, fish, and burgers are classics.

For vegetarian options, you can grill marinated tofu, portobello mushrooms, halved eggplants, zucchini, sweet potato, vegetable skewers, or corn ribs.

You can even grill fruit, such as peaches or watermelon!

Sides that go great with barbecues include potato salad, pasta salad, corn on the cob, coleslaw, potato chips, French fries, mac and cheese, chicken salad, sliders, and so much more!

TIPS

- Try to flip your food as little as possible – ideally, only once.
- Don't squeeze fatty or juicy foods like meat or vegetables over the grill unless you want them to be dry and crispy.

- Oil the grate periodically as you take things off the fire and put new ones on instead.
- Because the grill is so hot, your food will keep cooking for a bit even after you take it off – so you can slightly undercook your food to get that perfect doneness.

PART 7: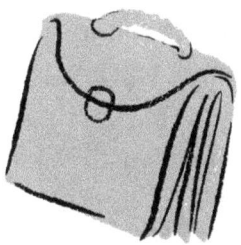
WORKING

CHAPTER 32:
WRITING A RÉSUMÉ

As a teenager, you are starting to become more independent. You might take on more responsibilities at home or at school, and in general, you are freer to make your own choices than you were as a child.

A big part of gaining independence is finding a job. Not only will working provide you with valuable experience for the future, but it will also grant you an income that is entirely your own. Whether you want to save for college or simply want some spending money of your own, the first step towards finding a job is writing your résumé.

A résumé is a short document, usually up to a page long, which includes all the information about you that could be relevant for a potential employer or hiring manager to know.

As a teen looking for your first "real" job, you may not have much to put on a résumé, but there are tricks to make your résumé stand out among others.

WHAT IS INCLUDED IN A RÉSUMÉ?

- **PERSONAL DETAILS:** At the top of the page, put your full name and your address.

- **CONTACT INFORMATION:** Your phone number and e-mail address, so that hiring managers can get in touch with you.

- **EDUCATION AND QUALIFICATIONS:** List the name of your high school and your (expected) graduation year.

If you have a GED, put that down too. If not, you can include your GPA. Include your major if it is related to the job you are applying for.

Also include any and all school activities and accomplishments, such as Honor Roll or school awards.

If you are a college student, list the name of your college and your expected graduation year.

- **QUALIFICATIONS:** If you have taken any extracurricular or out-of-school courses or training, you can list these too, including the name of the establishment and details of any certificate you may have received.

- **EXPERIENCE:** This section is where potential employers look for information on previous jobs and titles you've held to gauge your experience. This is where things might get tricky, as you may not have much work experience to lean on.

  If you have worked before, even informally as a babysitter, tutor, etc., be sure to include these jobs here. Add details about the responsibilities you had and the skills you acquired.

  In addition to work, you can add extracurricular activities you led or participated in at school, such as committees, clubs, sports teams, student government, events you planned, etc. This can show a future employee that you are well-rounded, hardworking, and take initiative.

- **SKILLS:** This is the place to write down any other abilities you may have that could help you excel at the job you're applying for. This could be computer proficiency, programming, graphic design, leadership, problem-solving, customer service, etc. Remember that anything a hiring manager reads in your résumé can come up in a subsequent interview, so only list skills that you feel comfortable elaborating on.

- **LANGUAGES:** Another section that can be found on most résumés is the language section, although some people include this information under "skills". Here, note the language or languages you speak, and your level of proficiency. Use these levels as a guide:

    Intermediate – you can understand and participate in basic conversation, but not well enough to converse freely.

    Advanced – you can carry out full conversations but speaking the language does not come completely naturally and you may lack some vocabulary or have an imperfect grasp of the grammar.

    Proficient – you speak the language fluently, though it is not your mother tongue.

    Native – this is your native language, which you have spoken from birth. If you are bilingual, list both languages as native.

HOW TO DESIGN A RÉSUMÉ

Résumés should be visually pleasing, so don't just type everything out in black and white. There are plenty of resources online where you can find free downloadable résumé templates, or you can design your own.

KEEP THESE GUIDELINES IN MIND:

- Choose a font that looks professional and is easy to read. Avoid cursive or childish fonts.

- Make sure your résumé is in a printable format and mobile-friendly.

- Choose a color scheme that is minimalistic and professional-looking.

- Keep it short and to the point – your résumé should not exceed one page.

CHAPTER 33:

FINDING A JOB

Once your resume is polished to perfection, you're ready for the next important step – finding a job. Besides making an income, having a job can help you develop important and useful skills, enrich your knowledge and experience, and kickstart your future career. It can also teach you responsibility, accountability, and independence.

The first step towards finding the perfect job for you is figuring out what kind of work interests you. Different people like different things, and not every job is suitable for everyone.

Start with some research – what kinds of jobs do your friends, siblings, and parents hold? Do you have a hobby or passion that you can convert into a job?

Here is a list of some good jobs for teenagers to get you thinking. Some, like being a lifeguard or working in a daycare, require prior knowledge, training, or talents.

- Grocery store cashier
- Restaurant server or host/hostess
- Fast food server or barista
- Lifeguard
- Retail associate
- Construction worker

- Dog walker
- Babysitter
- Private tutor
- Camp counselor
- Daycare assistant
- Start a business venture

You can also consider finding an online job – these are usually flexible and pay per hour, which makes them particularly attractive to busy teens:

- Creating social media content
- Selling your art online
- Completing surveys
- Participating in online experiments

Next, think about how much time you have available for a job. You might have just finished the school year and are looking for a full-time seasonal summer job for the next two months. Or maybe you're looking for part-time work you can do a few days a week after school. Perhaps you're looking only for a weekend job, or you're taking a gap year before college and want to work full-time. You might also consider working freelance – which is completely on your own time.

It's important to figure this out before you start applying for positions that may not be suited to your availability.

Once you have an idea of what you want to do and how available you are to do it, it's time to get out there and look for work! Being proactive is the best way to find a job, especially if you're looking to start as soon as possible.

Nowadays, social media is a great place to start your job hunt. Let your friends and family know what kind of job you're looking for and ask them if they know of any open positions that might suit you. This can pave the way to lots of exciting opportunities – and it also means you can get inside information on a potential position that someone you're close with may know a lot about.

If there's a specific field of work you're interested in, like working with animals or in a bakery, you can apply personally to relevant businesses in your area. Check with local businesses to see if they're hiring or send your resume by email along with details on your availability.

There are also plenty of online resources that pull together job listings which you can search by distance, occupation, and employment terms. Some of these websites even allow you to apply directly through an online form, making the process that much easier.

Don't be afraid to apply for more than one job at a time – having a selection of different options open to you can help you choose the job and conditions that will benefit you most.

Remember that you can always consult with your parents, teachers, older siblings, or another trusted adult with experience in the workforce. They might have useful insights and even connections to boost your search for a job!

CHAPTER 34:

ACING AN INTERVIEW

After perfecting your CV, it's time to start applying for job positions. In addition to a résumé with appropriate credentials, most jobs will require an interview (or more than one) before they accept candidates.

It doesn't matter if you're applying for a retail job, a job in the food industry, or an internship – you want to ace your interview and leave your interviewer with a great impression that will stand out among the pool of candidates they are sure to meet.

DO YOUR HOMEWORK

Before your interview, put some time and effort into researching the company, its values, and its history. This will both help you see how good a fit the job is for you and will demonstrate that you are thorough and resourceful, two positive qualities in a potential hire.

You can use Google to search for information or even visit the business's location to scout out its work environment and current focus. Contacting current or former employees, if you know any, is also a great way to gain insight into the job you're pursuing.

The job description you originally responded to might also hold clues as to the kind of employee the business is looking for. In addition to experience and skills, it may list qualities and other requirements that you can use to your benefit during the interview.

BE PREPARED

Spend some time thinking about answers to questions you may be asked in an interview and write them down to go over again several times before the interview. Even ask a family member or a friend to sit with you and simulate a job interview. If you've practiced beforehand, expressing yourself will come easier in real time.

THESE ARE SOME COMMON INTERVIEW QUESTIONS YOU CAN PREPARE FOR IN ADVANCE:

- **WHICH RELEVANT EXPERIENCE DO YOU HAVE?**

    List any previous experience that may give you an advantage over other candidates. You don't necessarily need to have worked in the same job or industry, but you might have worked or volunteered somewhere that taught you to be organized, or improved your ability to manage, and so on.

- **WHAT ARE YOUR STRENGTHS AND WEAKNESSES?**

    When listing your strengths, choose qualities that are relevant to the job you are after. These can be things like responsibility, thoroughness, work ethic, quick learning, etc. Leave out personal strengths that will not be an asset in the workplace.

    Similarly, when listing your weaknesses, avoid anything that might diminish your ability to do the job you are applying for. Opt for real weaknesses you see in yourself, which should be minimally detrimental to your character in the workplace.

- **WHAT WILL YOU CONTRIBUTE TO THIS WORKPLACE?**

  Your answer should convince the interviewer that you would be a real asset to the team. This is the place to point out any unique attributes, personality traits, and experience which would make you a perfect fit for the job.

- **TELL ME ABOUT A TIME WHEN YOU…**

  Your interviewer might want to hear about challenges you've overcome, successes you've experienced, times you've failed, projects you've led, etc. It can be difficult to remember these things when you're put on the spot, so try to think of a few interesting stories from your past experience to have ready.

MAKE AN IMPRESSION

How you look is a big part of the first impression you make. In fact, first impressions are believed to be formed within the first few seconds of meeting someone, which will often be over before you've even had a chance to open your mouth and introduce yourself.

- **DRESS SMART** – even if the job is in a casual setting, looking sharp at the interview is important. Avoid T-shirts and ripped or overly revealing clothes and put an effort into making your outfit look professional.

- **BE WELL-MANNERED** – shake your interviewer's hand, smile, and speak politely. Sit up straight and look them in the eyes, pay close attention to what is said, and show that you are pleasant to be around, an essential thing for an employer to see.

Remember – any interview, even an unsuccessful one, is an opportunity to learn! Ask for feedback or simply debrief yourself afterward, thinking about what you might do better next time.

CHAPTER 35:
UNDERSTANDING YOUR PAYCHECK

Anyone who is employed regularly by an employer should receive a paycheck in return for the work they have done. A paycheck can be a physical check that needs to be cashed in at the bank or a money transfer that goes directly into your bank account. Paychecks are paid periodically, every *pay period*, as detailed in your employment contract. A pay period typically ranges between a week and a month.

DIFFERENT TYPES OF EMPLOYEES

Some employees are employed with a fixed salary. They can be employed full-time (9-5, five days a week) or part-time (which is usually how teenagers who are still at school will be employed). Fixed salary employees will receive a fixed sum every pay period, with minimal changes.

Hourly employees, on the other hand, get paid a fixed salary for every hour that they work during a pay period. This means that their paycheck can change significantly from period to period, depending on how many hours of work they put in that week or month.

Hourly employment is popular among teenagers, as it is generally more flexible work which goes well with the busy schedule and varying availability that are characteristic of a teen's year.

PAY STUB

Together with your paycheck, you should receive a pay stub or slip. These are documents that show you the details of the salary you've just been paid – how many days or hours you worked, how much money you earned (your *gross income*, calculated according to your fixed salary or the hours you worked), how much money was deducted from your paycheck (due to tax, benefits, health insurance, sick leave, etc.), and your *net earnings*, which is your "take-home" pay, or the money that you'll receive after deductions.

Your pay stub will also detail how much PTO (paid time off) and sick days you have at your disposal, if any.

WITHHOLDING AND DEDUCTIONS

There are all sorts of payroll deductions you may see come up on your pay stub, and it's important to know what they all mean.

INCOME TAX: this is a tax that is paid to the state or government by any person or business that is making money. A portion of every payment you receive will be allocated to income tax, which is calculated based on your salary. In simple terms, the higher your salary – the more income tax you will pay.

401(K): a 401(k) is a popular retirement savings plan offered by many employers in the US. Once you reach retirement age, you will most likely no longer be working and making an income. A retirement plan is a way to ensure from a young age that you are putting away some of your money for safekeeping, to be used after your retirement. Every pay period, part of your salary is put into a retirement plan, and your employer might add a contribution of their own – up to or equaling the amount you contribute yourself.

HEALTH INSURANCE: many employers offer their employees healthcare plans. Your employer will decide which healthcare plan to provide and what it includes, and you and they will typically both contribute to the insurance premium payments. So, if you see some of your salary being deducted for the sake of health care, you can assume that your employer is contributing as well.

You can go back to chapter 20, *Taxes*, to learn more about the different types of taxes people pay.

When you pursue job opportunities, you will be told how much money you will earn. Keep in mind that you will probably be given a gross salary offer – so after taxes and other deductions, your net earnings will be somewhat lower.

CONCLUSION

If you've reached the end of this book, whether you've read every word or jumped between the chapters you thought would benefit you most, we're happy to have been able to provide you with some essential life skills as you set out to face the big wide world.

There is so much to learn about life and so many skills that you have yet to master on your own, but we believe that the skills thoughtfully and simply laid out in this book are invaluable sources of knowledge for young people. You are just starting your life – starting to learn who you are, to understand what you like and what kind of choices you should make, and perhaps making plans and dreams for your future. We hope that this book has taken you to a great starting point, and made you feel confident and capable in your abilities.

We know that growing up can sometimes come with pressure, anxiety, and a lot of uncertainty. It's important to remember that there are people around you who want the best for you – and can help you manage these feelings. After all, every adult was in your position once; excited to discover what the world has to offer, but perhaps unsure just how to start.

We ask that you take what you've learned from this book and use it to do good. Be a responsible citizen, a healthy and well-balanced adult, and a socially active and thoughtful human. You can keep *Essential Life Skills for Teen Boys* handy for whenever you need to go back and refresh your memory on how to prepare for a camping trip, what the deal is with taxes, how to do the laundry, or what the correct steps are for ironing a shirt.

We hope you've enjoyed this book and that it continues to be your guide, lighting your way through those wonderful teenage years.

THANK YOU SO MUCH FOR READING!

We'd appreciate your help and support so that we can keep bringing you more beautiful content like this, so if you could go to Amazon and leave us a review we'd be so grateful!

ABOUT MADE EASY PRESS

At **MADE EASY PRESS**, our goal is to bring you beautifully designed, thoughtful gifts and products.

We strive to make complicated things – easy. Whether it's learning new skills or putting memories into words, our books are led by values of family, creativity, and self-care and we take joy in creating authentic experiences that make people truly happy.

Look out for other books by **MADE EASY PRESS** here!

ABOUT THE AUTHOR

DANI SILAS wrote the *Essential Life Skills* series to help kids and teens acquire the self-confidence and independence to be the best they can be.

She believes that while school can teach you many important things, the *most* important things you can learn in life are the ones you learn outside the classroom. That's why the *Essential Life Skills* books are packed full of information, tips, and practical advice on everything from cooking and cleaning to social skills and handling money.

Dani loves to read and spend time with her husband and their dog, Amy. She studied psychology and linguistics and some of her favorite things are sunshine, Harry Potter, art, baking, and crafting.

www.ingramcontent.com/pod-product-compliance
Lightning Source LLC
LaVergne TN
LVHW020429070526
838199LV00004B/331